P9-BYF-230

Dress Your House for Success

Dress Your House for Success

5 Fast, Easy Steps to Selling Your House, Apartment, or Condo for the Highest Possible Price!

MARTHA WEBB
AND
SARAH PARSONS ZACKHEIM

THREE RIVERS PRESS
NEW YORK

Copyright © 1997 by Martha Webb and Sarah Parsons Zackheim

All rights reserved. No part of this book may be reproduced or transmitted in any form or by any means, electronic or mechanical, including photocopying, recording, or by any information storage and retrieval system, without permission in writing from the publisher.

Published by Three Rivers Press, New York, New York.
Member of the Crown Publishing Group.

Random House, Inc. New York, Toronto, London, Sydney, Auckland
www.randomhouse.com

THREE RIVERS PRESS is a registered trademark and the Three Rivers Press colophon is a trademark of Random House, Inc.

DYNAMIZING is a trademark of BCW^2 Corporation. All rights reserved.

Printed in the United States of America

Design by Lisa Sloane

Library of Congress Cataloging-in-Publication Data is available upon request.

ISBN 0-517-88844-0

15 14 13 12

TO BRUCE CLARK

my best friend, forever.

And

TO MY PARENTS

who lovingly taught me "good enough" isn't.

M. W.

ACKNOWLEDGMENTS

As this book took shape, so too did a friendship based on shared vision and dedication. The authors gratefully acknowledge each other's unique talents.

There are many people who played a role in bringing this book to life.

Martha thanks Margie, Paula, David, Jason, and Whitney for their help in countless moves and their celebration of this book; David Webb and Rick Webb for being all that brothers can be; Mary Kath, my first partner in Dynamizing; Joan Easton for facilitating a new friendship; Alice Title, who helped run a business while we wrote; Mickey O'Kane for connecting me to true artists; and all of the researchers—thousands of loyal customers who have provided feedback over the years.

A big thank you to David Gernert, who believed in this book from the beginning and supplied encouragement when it was in short supply; and Pam Krauss, whose keen editorial eye and gracious professionalism enhanced the book.

Finally, Sarah wishes to thank Alex and David, who helped in every possible way while their mom was hard at work; Adrian, who shared my joy in this project and much, much more; Peggy Kamins and Kim Reiter, whose friendships made the impossible, possible; and Nicholas Latimer, a true and loyal friend.

CONTENTS

Dress Your House for Success

INTRODUCTION

When selling a house, we all have the same goal—to sell it quickly and at the highest price possible. Since 1970, eight of my homes have sold—each in a matter of days—at full asking price. In fact, my last two homes sold in less than four hours at prices of $12,500 to $17,500 over what market experts had predicted I would receive. I have also helped friends, relatives, and neighbors sell their homes . . . with the same great results. And they are continually stunned at how magnificent and inviting their homes look and feel when I'm done. But what pleases them most is how quickly their houses sell, and for top dollar, too!

The idea of sharing my homeselling secrets came to me in 1988 after I had sold my seventh house. By then, I had streamlined my homeselling strategy. I began by asking several real estate agents to recommend a listing price for my house. They each toured the house, worked up a competitive market analysis, and then arrived at virtually the same price—a figure only slightly higher than what I had paid for the house two years earlier! I was disheartened but determined to realize a good profit on the time and money I'd spent updating the house. The agents had toured the house early on, before my work was complete. I knew the appeal of the house and I just knew it would bring a higher price. I had listened to friends and neighbors exclaim how they loved my house, and I was determined to get back every penny I'd put in—and more. I asked my agent to give me some time to get the house into selling condition, and then reconsider his recommended listing price. When the house was ready for market, he couldn't believe what he saw and we agreed to list it at the very, very top of the price range. Two hours into the first Open House, he called to tell me I had an offer— $12,500 over the first price recommendation.

With my substantial profit in hand, I asked my agent what he thought made the difference between the price he first expected the house to sell for and the actual sale price. He said, without a doubt, the increased sale price was due to how carefully I had prepared the house for sale: "Most people don't understand how critical this is to a successful sale." His answer started me really thinking—about the vast amount of money going untapped, and about how I could help other homesellers experience the same financial success that I have had.

After that conversation, I started to write down exactly what I did to houses to produce such great sales results. As I wrote, I began to realize that my homeselling success was due to how I used my career experience—over ten years in film production and motivational communications—to stage houses. I began to see that my approach was unique. I'm sure not many other homesellers approached each room in their house as if the doorframe were a camera lens. The "photograph" you take—a buyer's first glimpse of the room—forms the first impression of that room or area. As in advertising or motivational communications, you have only a few critical seconds to make a positive impression. I realized I was "controlling" the feelings and attitudes of home buyers in much the same way I did when producing motivational programs for clients—and the results of my "home staging" were powerful. I worked to ensure that each room made a potential buyer want to stay and generated a positive feeling that remained imprinted in his mind long after the visit.

In 1989, I founded a company, BCW Video, to produce and distribute video marketing tools. After a year of research, we introduced the video "Dress Your House For Success." While the concept of preparing a house for sale was not new, the specific motivational and staging elements I introduced were instantly embraced by the real estate industry. Now, the video is *the* best-selling video in the industry. It has won the acclaim of top real estate professionals across the United States and Canada, and it has helped tens of thousands of homeowners sell their homes quickly and profitably. Real estate agents rave that my program works for absolutely every house—in all price ranges and all styles.

There is no magic to dressing your house for success. Anyone can do it with the same great results I enjoy each and every time. This book will not only tell you how, it will *show* you how. Of course, we all know that the better a house looks, the quicker it will probably sell. However, if I tell you to "clean your house," you may think only in terms of what you *normally* do to clean your house. If I tell you specifically that cleaning means using glass cleaner on the inside and outside of your glass fireplace doors, scrubbing the inside of cupboards, even cleaning the pipes that go from the bathroom sink to the wall, then you begin to get the picture. But even the most thorough cleaning alone won't help you realize the kind of financial success that lies in store when you use my program. The real secret is "Dynamizing," staging rooms to generate feelings—in every area and around every corner—that make buyers feel a visceral connection to your house.

As an added bonus, setting the stage of your home not only makes for a great sale, it provides an unbeatable send-off for the next chapter of your life. You'll be organized as never before and ready to move on. Instead of bogging down in the drudgery of moving and packing and unpacking, you can concentrate on the excitement of a new place and the new life you and your family will make there.

The plan to help you get organized is easy to follow and doesn't require a big financial investment. So start filling out those change-of-address forms—with my five-step program as your guide, you can be ready to sell your house profitably, in only ten days, or less!

—*Martha Webb*

1

THE BASICS OF
HOMESELLING SUCCESS

IF YOU'VE EVER placed a house, condominium, or apartment on the market, you know the thrill of receiving that first offer. You may also know how disheartening it is if that offer is disappointingly low or doesn't come in for weeks, months, or more. Or, maybe you've experienced the frustration of having lots of people go through your house without receiving a single offer. It makes you start to wonder . . . and worry.

Many times, real estate agents have told me about sellers poised to lower their price to attract buyers before they learned about my Dress Your House for Success program. Guess what? As soon as they completed the five easy steps, the house sold, often for full price, or more. Every type and size of house imaginable, from cabins and cottages to single-family homes and mansions, can be prepared to reap immediate and profitable results from this ten-day plan.

> **Every house will sell . . . it's a matter of when and for how much.**

When I sold my first house—even my second—I was not aware that, as the seller, you have a great deal of control over your success in the housing market, even the ability to price it at the very highest end of your price range. Unearthing the hidden pocket of money—$10,000 to $20,000 or more!—that exists in your house is easy if you know how to look for it. I've done it time and time again, and so can you.

There's a windfall in every house.

TURN HOUSE-HUNTERS INTO HOME BUYERS

People begin house-hunting in a very logical state of mind, but ultimately they buy a home for emotional reasons. Home buying begins with house-hunting, but emotion— the feelings and desire for a comfortable home and lifestyle— propels buyers to purchase a specific house.

Perhaps the easiest way to understand the mind-set and motivation of a buyer is to think about your own experiences of purchasing or renting a home. Can you remember what it was that prompted you to commit? Clutching a list of desirable features, you looked at dozens of houses that more or less fit your criteria . . . but none of them were just right. When you least expected it, though, it happened. Within minutes, you knew this was the *one,* and the other houses previously viewed seemed insignificant in comparison. You were overtaken by a powerful feeling: I belong here.

Buyers look at an average of twelve houses in an eight- week period.

THE THREE STAGES OF BUYING

Buyers move through three stages in buying a home. Stage one usually begins before they actually look at houses. They do their homework; they narrow down the location, the price range (many of today's savvy buyers may go through a mortgage preapproval), and the style and size of their next house. Stage two, then, begins when the buyers arrive to objectively view your property so they can begin to evaluate how it fits their particular needs.

> Only if buyers "feel" as if your house could be home can they determine if it will be.

Progressing through stage two requires buyers to *feel* an emotional sense of *home* in your house. Whether a buyer experiences those feelings or not depends entirely on how you prepare your house. When a buyer's heart says, "This is it . . . this is the one . . . this is *home*," he moves to stage three: purchase negotiations.

I remember house-hunting with my three small children when that magical recognition of "home" first happened to me. Our real estate agent was driving us to look at a house that he knew fit my needs perfectly. Everything on my "must have" list

> Love at first sight.

checked out: three bedrooms, two bathrooms, a first-floor family room and den, a two-car garage, *and* it was located in a great family neighborhood.

Yet we never got to that house because, as we drove, I spotted a house out the car window with a FOR SALE sign. Its appeal was so strong that I asked the agent to stop. I could hardly contain my enthusiasm and excitement. The anticipation built as the agent arranged for a showing, and when I finally approached the front door, I kept a mental list of each little aspect that I loved: the landscaping, the bay window, the brick exterior, the outdoor lighting fixtures. I walked into the living room, looked at the fireplace, then moved into the dining room with its two beautiful built-in china cabinets. The house hunt was over. I had found our home. Aloud, I said, "I want it."

Even without its fulfilling my specific checklist of needs, this was exactly the type of home I had pictured for my young family. To adapt the space to our needs would take a little work. Even though it had only one and a half baths, a recreation room in the basement, and a single-car garage, I was willing to compromise because of its charm. With so much space and character in the upstairs bedroom, I could easily imagine the kids having a great time living and playing in it. Although the recreation room was in the basement, it had been remodeled with quality materials and tastefully decorated and was larger than most first-floor family rooms. It even had a fireplace and an extra finished room that I envisioned as a great hobby area. As a bonus, the house boasted a quaint breezeway that looked ideal for casual entertaining, diminishing the importance of a family room.

> **When a house feels as if it could be home, buyers will intuitively reprioritize their list.**

This house "felt" like the perfect gathering place for my family and friends. It reminded me of how much I loved to entertain and how I hadn't done so lately because my previous house simply didn't have the space. Once-important features on my "must have" list were replaced with items I hadn't even realized I wanted. Yet once I saw those features, they—and the lifestyle they represented—were so compelling to me that I knew I had to have this house.

A few months later when we were moving in, I was unpacking in the master bedroom and came across a box of dishes, which I asked my daughters to put in the dishwasher. They came back after what seemed like a long time and said, "Mom, there isn't a dishwasher anywhere." I stopped what I was doing. Had I really fallen so in love with the house that I bought it without carefully checking the kitchen appliances? How could I have overlooked a dishwasher? Was I crazy?

No, I wasn't crazy. In fact, we all sat there on the floor laughing because we realized it didn't make any difference. We loved this house. It contained something much more important than a dishwasher . . . or any specific feature. It had touched me emotionally and inspired me to think about how the house could enrich my family life. I *felt* good in the house. In the eight years we lived there, we remodeled the kitchen (to include a dishwasher!), converted a first-floor bedroom into a family room, and added a two-car garage. While we eventually outgrew the house, my children and I still remember it as one of our best homes. It absolutely lived up to the "promise" I felt the moment I saw it.

As a buyer there's nothing like the feeling of knowing a house is right. Nine out of ten home sales are a result of that feeling. Your goal as a seller is generating that *feeling of home* to facilitate a quick sale and put money in your pocket.

YOUR PARTNER: THE REAL ESTATE AGENT

A homeselling experience should go quickly, smoothly, and profitably with all of my techniques, whether you are selling your home yourself or are teaming up with a real estate professional. I have sold houses both with and without real estate agents and found it extremely stressful and time-consuming to go it alone. If you think you might want to try selling your house yourself, take a moment to look realistically at what's involved. Ask yourself the following questions:

> **When your house is ready, make sure it plays to the largest audience.**

- Can I afford the time it could take to sell my house with only a sign in the yard and an ad in the local paper? Research shows that 50 percent of buyers hear about a house through an agent, not an advertisement. Without access to those buyers, a sale could take twice as long.

- Am I able to stay at home to take calls and conduct tours? Do I know how to screen inquiries so as not to waste precious time showing my house to unqualified buyers?

- Do I know what to do before putting a house on the market (disclosure laws or local inspection regulations)? Will I know what to do when someone says, "I want to buy your house"? Do I have the necessary legal and financial knowledge to answer buyers' questions, negotiate a contract, and close a sale?

SELECTING THE RIGHT AGENT

Use these guidelines to select a real estate professional.

✔ Talk with friends, neighbors, and coworkers who recently sold in your area. Whom did they work with, and were they happy? Would they use this agent or company again?

✔ Go to open houses in your area and observe the listing agents. Do you like the way they are marketing the house? How knowledgeable are they about the house and the market? Are you comfortable with the answers they have to your questions? Are you impressed with their professionalism?

✔ Take note of SOLD signs in your area. This is a sure indication of an active, successful agent.

✔ Interview at least three agents. Try to find out as much about each as possible. Because you will be working closely together, you want to be absolutely certain that you are comfortable with your agent's style of doing business. Here are some important questions to ask:

1. What are your qualifications, experience, and education?

2. How long have you been selling real estate? How long in this area?

3. What is your track record? How many houses have you sold in the last three months? Will you supply three references from these recent sales?

4. How will you find buyers for my house? May I see a marketing proposal? Are you connected to a relocation network? (Access to out-of-town buyers and corporate transferees substantially increases the pool of potential buyers.)

5. What if I am not satisfied with your service?

If you answered yes to all these, selling your house yourself might be an option. If you have any hesitation, interview a few agents before deciding (see page 23). There is a good reason why 80 percent of all houses sold are sold through real estate professionals. A good real estate agent can be a vital ally and partner, and her experience, understanding of the market, and connection to other real estate services can make a sale go much more smoothly.

An agent can give your house exposure through the Multiple Listing Service; assist you with strategic pricing; screen buyers; show your home; negotiate the best sale; and facilitate the closing. However, only you can determine how your house will ultimately be positioned in the buyers' minds. Above all, keep in mind that this is your show. You are the one in charge of your homeselling success.

> **This is your show. With or without an agent, *you* determine your house's position.**

VARIABLE CONDITIONS THAT AFFECT SALES

At any given time, three general factors affect the sale of your house: the current real estate market conditions, the location of your property, and the competition—other houses like yours competing for the same buyers. These three factors are always in flux. For example, interest rates rise and fall; neighborhoods lose or gain cachet; similar houses suddenly arrive on the market; and the pool of active buyers changes. No one can control these factors, and you cannot wait until all the conditions are absolutely perfect to sell your house. Smart sellers don't put themselves at the mercy of these factors —they maximize conditions to their advantage.

The Market

Packaging will make your property stand out from the competition whether the market is booming or not. In a buyer's market (where there are more houses than buyers), preparing and dressing your home is the best way to make it memorable and easy for buyers to recall at the end of a long day of house-hunting. When buyers have a greater selection to choose from, your competition will have to measure up to your house. Likewise, in a seller's market (where there are more buyers than houses) great packaging will make your house appeal to many buyers, drawing out the highest possible price. Receiving multiple bids can push your selling price higher.

A close friend recently discovered that acquaintances of hers were moving out of town, and she asked if she could purchase their house when they were ready to sell. All predeal conversations were amicable, but the asking price was just a little higher than my friend could pay. Instead of losing out on this opportunity to move to a nicer house, she decided to put her own house on the market—to see if it would bring enough to allow her to purchase her dream home. Anxious to get top dollar, she followed my program to a tee and, during her first weekend on the market,

> **Dressing your house can help you buy your dream home.**

received not one but three offers. The third offer was $10,000 over the asking price—$25,000 more than market experts who saw the house in "as is" condition told her she could hope to receive.

Location

Trite as is sounds, "location, location, location" is important, and if your house is in a less-than-ideal location, you can't move it. To make the most of it, turn your house into the most appealing house in that location.

On the other hand, if your neighborhood is desirable, the competition is even keener, so packaging your house properly will put it ahead of the rest. Remember, if your house doesn't stand out, another will, and it will get top dollar. By not preparing your house, you're simply making the competition look better—you're helping sell their house!

> Leaving your house in "as is" condition can help sell the competition.

Competition

When a number of houses with similar features are on the market, yours needs to shine. If two houses are similar in structure or layout, buyers will choose the one that feels as if it could be home.

A few years ago a friend needed to sell her town house under less than ideal conditions. The market was soft. Interest rates were high. There were three other town houses for sale in the same complex that had all been substantially improved, yet weren't priced much higher than she wanted to price hers.

To make matters worse, she had recently divorced and the town house had a half-lived-in look and feel that reflected her current state of affairs: disarray. We rolled up our sleeves and worked to position her town house as a home. It sold before any of the other more improved units and at full price! Dressing her town house for success was clearly a case of outsmarting the competition.

> **If two houses are similar, buyers will choose the one that touches them emotionally.**

THE ART OF PRICING

Pricing a house for market is much more of an art than a science. There isn't an exact formula to help you arrive at the magic number. Likewise, no magic number exists as the "right" price for your house, simply a range within which the sale price of your house will fall. Why? Because houses are a commodity subject to the laws of supply and demand, and market conditions keep changing. Prices rise when there are more buyers than sellers; they decline when there are more houses for sale than buyers. The availability of mortgage money also affects sales, but ultimately what the buyer feels about a house is what determines the price he'll pay.

> **A well-priced home is half-sold.**

While the buyer determines the *selling* price, *you* establish the *listing* price of your house. To arrive at a realistic listing price, research your competition's pricing. Find out what similar houses have sold for recently as well as what "comparables" haven't sold to give you a good idea of the price buyers are and are not willing to pay for houses similar to yours. While it's difficult to pinpoint exactly what helped sell or not sell a house, comparing other prices will give you a realistic idea of how high you can set your price. Remember, a buyer will be looking at a number of houses with similar features and amenities.

Ask your agent to prepare a competitive market analysis for you and check recent real estate transactions in your area. All of this research provides a very real look at current sales activity including which houses are vying for the same buyers you are, what houses sold recently, and what houses haven't sold. Assembling this information will show you what today's pool of buyers are buying and what they're not. Recognize, too, that the houses that aren't selling are probably overpriced or underdressed.

Your competition will clue you into what buyers are willing to pay.

For the most accurate, realistic pricing range, I find it extremely helpful to actually go out and tour houses that are for sale. Looking at a listing sheet or data table that itemizes the square footage and number of bedrooms, bathrooms, and fireplaces is nothing like actually seeing the whole property. Only then can I visualize how their features stack up to my own house's assets. I gain a much better perspective on the competition and its pricing when I personally see and evaluate each house's features and *condition*.

The market determines your price range. You determine where your house falls within that range.

Usually the specific features in your house will determine its price range. For example, a three-bedroom, one-bath house in a certain neighborhood will sell for less than a three-bedroom, two-bath house in the same neighborhood, because buyers are willing to pay more for a second bathroom. However, there are also features that people aren't willing to pay extra for. For example, two identical houses are for sale right next to each other. One owner has had problems with the foundation and has been forced to spend money on correcting the problem. He would like to get his money back and adds his repair costs to his selling price. The result: two identical houses at different prices. Buyers, though, expect a house to have a solid foundation. They aren't willing to pay more for a house just because the owner wants to recoup his repair costs. To a buyer, both houses are structurally sound. One is overpriced and will be rejected.

Be prepared—pricing is emotional. Imagine putting a dollar figure on your personal values and your memories. To you, your house represents both a tangible and intangible asset, a personal reflection and culmination of the many facets of your life. Many sellers find it frustrating—are even offended—if the market value of their house doesn't reflect their emotional and personal attachment. It helps to be realistic about the features buyers won't pay for—your memories don't qualify as a feature, although pulling at *buyers'* emotions in your packaging

> **The sentimental value of a house is only in the memories it has provided for its owners. To a buyer, a house is just a commodity.**

will make a difference. While buyers aren't necessarily looking for a real steal, they won't pay more than fair market value for a house.

Beware of overpricing your house, a dangerous tactic that often backfires because you lose the critical window of time—the first two weeks a house is on the market—when the most serious pool of buyers arrive ready to buy. These serious buyers have done their homework; they've shopped around; they have probably looked at several other houses before yours; and they know property values. They won't buy a house that's overpriced.

In fact, if you price your house too high, your competition looks like a better deal. Why help sell your competition?

Overpriced and underdressed can make your house a wallflower.

Instead, package and price your house to outshine the competition, to ensure you a spot at the very top of your price range. Even better, you might be able to push that range just a little bit higher by providing buyers with the best. People won't overpay, but they will pay a premium for *the best* on the market.

Your results in the homeselling market have nothing to do with luck. The responsibility ultimately rests with you to price and dress it to sell quickly and profitably.

2

SEEING WITH "BUYER'S EYES"

TO PACKAGE YOUR house in the best possible manner, start by thinking about how a buyer will look at your house. Think of the process as theater—you're putting your house on-stage! Just as a theater company wouldn't let a paying audience attend rehearsals, buyers should not see your house before it's ready. You want to *prepare* it for its big debut.

One vital asset in homeselling is your ability to acquire *buyer's eyes*—to actually see your house as your customer would. Buyer's eyes help a seller make memorable impressions by creating positive packaging in various areas of the house. Buyer's eyes also give you a realistic view of your house, enabling you to ask yourself such **Stepping back to see objectively is the first step toward success.** questions as: Is this what I want buyers to see? Is this how I want buyers to feel? Buyer's eyes let you evaluate whether your house will make a strong impact and encourage a sale or be prematurely crossed off a buyer's list as not quite right.

Understand that the way you actually live in your house is not the way you want it to look and *feel* when it's on the market.

Many sellers get defensive at this advice, but shouldn't take it personally—it's not a suggestion that the house is a mess or that the decorating is a nightmare. To position your house for the fresh, discriminating eyes of buyers, you'll need to look at it differently while it's on the market—as a product for sale—than you would when you're living in it.

Once, I lived in a house with a small upstairs bathroom that was used primarily by my children. It had gray wallpaper with a jungle pattern, and dated pink and gray tiles on the floor. When we moved into the house, I installed some new track lighting to brighten that bathroom a bit. The kids never seemed to mind the decor. With teenagers, my main concern was that it be kept reasonably clean. It was a *bathroom*, part of our home, a fixture in our lives.

After many happy years in that house, we decided to sell. With notepad in hand, I walked carefully through the house examining it through buyer's eyes. When I came to that little bathroom, I heard voices loud and clear in my head. The real estate agent cleared her throat. "Here's the second bath . . . great for kids," she said in a hurry to move on to some of the better features on the second floor. Worse, I could also hear my customer's mind working. "This bathroom! It's tiny. And these awful old tiles, that ugly, busy wallpaper. This is going to need work!" Without taking the time to brighten it up and make it more appealing, I would miss the opportunity to make a critical good first impression on an important feature—an additional bathroom.

Buyer's eyes help you see and "hear" your customer's reactions.

Buyer's eyes help you know what your customer is seeing and therefore how your house will be positioned in his mind. Even more than that, buyer's eyes can tell you how potential buyers will *feel* about your house. I knew right away that prospective buyers would be seeing and feeling the wrong thing when they saw that bathroom. Instead of "Isn't this small," I wanted them to think "This is adorable!" Instead of "How dated," I wanted them to exclaim "Charming!"

TOO CLOSE TO HOME

Your home is your haven. Almost as soon as you live in a house, you become less objective about it. Images of home include memories of family occasions and milestones, of raising children, entertaining friends, and sharing holidays. It is a world unto itself. No wonder it's difficult to separate the feelings you have about home from the house itself.

Because of that, we all live in our homes with blinders on. We don't see the cracked storm window. We stop seeing the missing tile in the bathroom and the chipped paint in the hall. We aren't irritated anymore by the loose doorknob. We're busy with life itself. We simply don't see our house with a critical eye.

If you can't see objectively, you can't package effectively.

In one of my homes, we had a wonderful little shoe cubbyhole in our front entry, which was a great way to keep boots and extra shoes out of the hall. My kids, however, thought it was a target and kicked their shoes into it, missing more often than not, creating lots of black shoe marks around the cubbyhole.

After a while I didn't even see them because when I came in the front door, I was flooded with feelings of "coming home." I was eager to see my family; my thoughts were not focused on the house—they were focused on my life.

> Our homes are part of our lives, and as with our children, we don't see all the faults.

However, for a potential buyer, the black shoe marks were the first thing she'd see when walking in my front door. Her first impression may be that the house hasn't been well cared for. Once those black shoe marks have made a negative impression, a smart buyer will probably be on the lookout for other types of wear and tear. When I got ready to sell this house, my buyer's eyes spotted that target instantly. I spent twenty-five minutes painting the shoe cubby with a fresh coat of white paint, and the immediate response from buyers was "What a cute little place for shoes!" That positive impression set the tone for the rest of the tour.

HOW TO GET BUYER'S EYES

Start by referring to your home as a "house." The word *house* carries much less of an emotional tie. Then, get out of your house and start to act like a buyer.

- ❏ **Go to open houses.** Watch how buyers go through a house. Take note of what they look at and how they talk about what they see. Listen for their emotional statements—both positive and negative. Also, take note of how the condition of the house makes *you* feel.

What are your first impressions

- as you drive up to the house?

- as you walk to the front door?

- of the entryway?

- of the kitchen?

- of the bathrooms?

- of the closet space?

Do you feel comfortable in the house? Examine why you do or don't.

❑ **Look at model homes.** These are professionally staged to appeal to buyers. Take special note of how a carefully staged house makes you *feel*. How do you feel in a house that is *completely clean:* no fingerprints on the walls, no grease stains by the stove, no toiletries with dust on them, no rain spots on windows. Notice how you respond to uncluttered rooms and closets. Notice, too,

**Step outside
to gain a
new perspective.**

the sense that there is no work to be done—no screens to repair, no walls to paint, no doorknobs or handles to tighten. This "model home effect" is exactly the look and feel you want to create in your customer's mind.

❑ **Read decorating and home magazines and catalogs.** Designers, stylists, and editors spend hours staging each room to get the details just so. Clip out specific furniture arrangements and propping that appeal to you. Think about the message that is being conveyed by each setting and the feelings it generates.

As you begin to explore houses, take note of little touches or specific rooms that you like—keep a notebook to record what you see that pleases your eye. Incorporate those ideas and copy them in your house as you prepare it for sale: If a little touch appeals to you or creates a sense of "home" for you, it will also work for someone like you. After all, chances are good that someone with tastes similar to yours will purchase your home.

TURNING NEGATIVES INTO POSITIVE IMPRESSIONS

No matter how many great elements you have in your house, people's eyes are drawn to negative features first. Buyers are "inspecting"—looking for clues to uncover hidden costs. Anxious to protect themselves, they seek reasons *not* to buy your house.

Once buyer's eyes have fastened on a negative feature, it's difficult for them to see beyond it. When buyers are greeted with clutter, they'll tour the house with the perception that it's small and not well maintained. They will probably also be looking for other signs of neglect because that first impression will have set a negative tone. Chances are, they'll walk away remembering the cramped and cluttered entryway. Whether the entryway is actu-

> Negatives cause buyers to stop looking for what's right with the house and start wondering, "What's wrong?"

ally small or not isn't the issue; what matters is the buyer's perceptions and feelings. Remember, because buyer's eyes are drawn to negatives first, they tend to exaggerate—in their minds—the amount of work required and the cost to overcome negative features.

No one is as uniquely qualified to package your house as you are because you know exactly what your house has to offer. This intimate knowledge can also be a huge handicap because our emotional attachment and associations with a house can actually prevent us from seeing it objectively through buyer's eyes. Ironically, you have to distance yourself emotionally in order to re-create a similar emotional tie—in the buyer! Once you do, you can create a package that is irresistible to buyers.

Any buyer coming to look at your house could be the one to purchase it, so you must package your house to appeal to the largest possible number of potential buyers. However, if there are negatives that keep a buyer from connecting emotionally to it, he will check your house off his list as "not right." If there are *too* many negatives, you may have to lower your price. To counteract these negatives, simply package your home so its strengths shine through. The more people who appreciate your house's strong points, the better your chances are for a quick and profitable sale. Remember, you're looking for only one buyer . . . you just don't know which one is *the one*.

> You only need one buyer, but no one ever knows which one it will be.

While preparing your house, you will be approaching every room with the question "Does it look like new?" If you find yourself answering "It looks good enough," then it probably doesn't. The Dress Your House for Success program is a layering of steps, each one building on the other, resulting in a house positioned for a quick and profitable sale. The first four steps— Uncluttering, Cleaning, Repairing, and Neutralizing—form the crucial foundation that allows buyers to see a roomy, clean, functional space in good repair. You will open possibilities by broadening your house's appeal.

MAKE THE FIRST IMPRESSION POSITIVE

It's *positive* impressions that will sell your house quickly and for the highest possible price. Transforming negative impressions into unforgettably positive ones will create a succession of positive images that position your house in the buyer's mind as the perfect place for her to enjoy the life she wants.

Real estate professionals know that home-buying decisions happen quickly—most buyers form an opinion of your house within fifteen seconds of that first glimpse. In fact, the "decision clock" for most home buyers starts running the moment they drive up to your house. If their first sight

The tone of a house tour can be set in a single glance.

is of weeds around foundation plantings, and buckling, peeling exterior paint, their first impression will be "There's work to be done here!" Remember, in touring your house the buyer will be on the lookout for more work or may immediately conclude that the house just isn't right.

When buyers are welcomed with an engagingly positive scene—an immaculate yard, window boxes bursting with beautiful blooms, freshly painted trim, and a polished door handle for that first touch—they'll begin the tour looking for how this house can fit their needs. If this engaging first impression is succeeded by positive impressions throughout, the house is as good as sold. You want your house to exude positive feelings of cleanliness and spaciousness from the moment buyers drive up, and to radiate the sense that all that awaits them is the pleasure of making themselves at home.

3

THE ART OF POSITIONING YOUR HOME

WHEN YOUR HOUSE is for sale, it is, first and foremost, a product, like the thousands of products for sale every day in grocery stores, shopping malls, and catalogs. Manufacturers go to great lengths to position their products correctly in the mind of their target audiences, using advertising, point-of-sale displays, pricing, and packaging to reach the consumer. Likewise, properly packaging your house will speed up the important shift in a buyer from seeing just a three-bedroom, two-bath house to seeing a *home* in which he begins to imagine himself living.

Marketing a house in "as is" condition—as far too many homesellers do—clouds how buyers see your house. As they walk from room to room, they peer in at your life and the way you live in the house. They may even feel uneasy, as if they're trespassing on your privacy. People cannot and should not be asked to see beyond your belongings to evaluate the house as a

It's hard for buyers to visualize it as *their* house if it's still *your* house.

potential future home. If you choose to sell your house without preparation, in "as is" condition, chances are it will remain both your house and on the market longer than you want—at least until a buyer who possesses a rare visualizing talent sees beyond what exists and appreciates the larger possibilities of what can be. Because "what it can be" usually entails work, time, and money, buyers are then less likely to pay top dollar.

Never leave it up to the buyer to do the visual work. Create powerful impact moments that buyers will respond to immediately, from the minute they drive up to your house to each time they enter a room. Creating not one or two, but twenty-five to thirty-five powerful, indelible first impressions that position your house as home is what enables you to sell it quickly and profitably.

Buyers believe they'll know the right house when they see it, as you probably did when you found your current house. Moving drains much energy and finances, so the less work your house needs, the better. However, this is not about major remodeling or redecorating, just simple packaging techniques—inexpensive and quick. Since other products consumers purchase come carefully packaged, a house—the most expensive product most will ever buy—should be no different.

THE HOMESELLER'S ADVANTAGE IS A MARKETER'S DREAM!

At your fingertips lie resources that the average marketer can only dream about. Marketers vie for the attention of their audience, whether on television or in the mall, with only one extremely brief chance—a few seconds—to capture the attention of their audience, make an impression, and close the sale.

Your situation is different . . . and better. You have the advantages of the following:

- ❑ **A perfectly targeted audience.** Most buyers who come to your house are good prospects (even "just curious" neighbors may tell a friend about your house): They are actively shopping for the product you are selling, whereas in other situations shoppers might need a variety of products or might not know exactly what they need. What's more, your house probably already meets their general criteria, determined before they arrive.

- ❑ **A captive audience.** The buyer is in your house and will spend up to an hour studying it. For that time, your house is the only product the buyer is focused on.

- ❑ **An opportunity to make multiple impressions.** Each room provides the perfect opportunity to make dozens of "first" impressions (every room, every nook and cranny), all directed at moving the buyer from looking at your house to evaluating whether it could be *home*.

THE SECRET: POSITIONING YOUR HOUSE AS "HOME"

When buyers experience the *feelings of home* in your house, they start to connect emotionally to it and begin to imagine what it would be like to live there. That emotional spark of feeling "at home" ignites a mental shift in buyers, who go from seeing "a house with three bedrooms"

> **In a well-positioned house, its features will shine through and convey the message of home.**

to the more personal thought that "this room would make a wonderful study," and "this room is perfect for Julia," etc. When buyers start to imagine entertaining in your dining room, playing pool in your rec room, even adding personal decorating touches, it's just a matter of time before they commit to a sale.

Facilitating a critical mental shift in the buyer's mind is called positioning. It's a marketing concept, described by Al Ries and Jack Trout in their book *Positioning*, that's so simple people often have trouble understanding how powerful it is. Positioning starts with a product, in this case, your house, but reflects what you do to the mind of the buyer rather than what you do with the product. Ideally, you position your house in the mind of your buyer as a home that will fill her specific needs or desires. Note that the house is not significantly changed through remodeling or redecorating. However, simply highlighting certain features will convey a message or feeling associated with "home."

> **Beauty, comfort, and harmony are elements of a home that often don't make the checklist, but are nonetheless "must haves."**

The house I mentioned on page 19 promised to be a perfect gathering place for entertaining family and friends because the seller positioned it that way. It had character and the kind of details that I knew I would enjoy decorating, with wonderful private spaces that made me feel as if I could pursue my own interests beyond just taking care of three small children. Everything seemed to have a place, and I felt that would help me be better organized. Even the laundry room looked neat and finished, promising less work and more living. Certainly I could relax in this house and at the same time enjoy more quality time with my children. Without knowing me, the savvy seller of that house positioned and packaged it well for a young, social family.

POSITIONING TO MAKE THE FEELING LAST

The most powerful package is made up of appealing impressions, and the four most critical first-impression areas are curb appeal, the term the real estate industry uses to describe the view from the curb; the entryway; the kitchen; and the bathrooms. Especially positive and inviting are a freshly painted facade, a roaring fire, light streaming through a window illuminating a fresh bouquet of flowers, plush bathroom towels and luxurious soaps, the elegance of a dining room that suggests pride in entertaining. The more pleasurable the impressions created, the longer buyers will want to stay in your house, and the more involved they'll become in considering it.

> Within fifteen seconds buyers develop an attitude toward your house that is reinforced by everything else they encounter.

As a visual communicator, I know that in only a few critical seconds you can capture an audience and communicate a message . . . or lose all their interest. Engaging the senses generates a feeling in the mind of the potential buyer. For example, you can create a vignette around an armchair in no time to position

your house as a place where one will have leisure time: Drape an afghan over the arm of the chair and plump up the cushions to invite people to sink in. Turn on a reading lamp to spotlight the area and place an open book on the table next to the chair.

By packaging this inviting little "nook," you've highlighted an area and elicited a feeling. This highlighting technique helps a buyer see important elements—like the relaxation and comfort your house offers—he may otherwise miss while rushing through looking for the features on his list. Now, he'll "see" relaxation the minute he walks in and will look at the rest of the room—and probably the house —from that perspective. Impression points slow down a buyer and get him actively involved in your home. He starts to *feel* the restful, cozy sensations of home that your package generates. More persuasively than by an agent's saying, "This is a wonderful place to relax and read," you are convincing the buyer that the people who live in this house have time to read—that your house will facilitate a relaxed, comfortable lifestyle. This message can't be conveyed by just a chair, a lamp, a table, and a book unless they're packaged to generate a *feeling*. Hollywood filmmakers and theater directors rely on this technique to "prop" for a film shoot and "set" a stage to generate a feeling. So too will you as you prepare your house for sale. Staging fuels the imagination of the buyer.

Impression points actively engage a buyer's mind to imagine how life can be in this house.

Help buyers remember your house as the one that felt like "coming home."

The main objective in triggering all these feelings is to make your house stand out memorably from similar houses on a buyer's list. A buyer will recall features of a house based on the feelings he experienced there. As a marketer, you can easily control exactly what buyers see, hear, smell, and recall, and thus ensure that your house is positively positioned and firmly imprinted in buyers' minds.

HOW LONG WILL IT TAKE TO DRESS YOUR HOUSE FOR SUCCESS?

The Dress Your House for Success program is designed to be accomplished over the course of ten days of intensive effort, and on the pages that follow, you'll see that I've allocated time for each of the five steps as follows: two days each for Uncluttering and Cleaning, three days for Repairing, two for Neutralizing, and the final day for Dynamizing. In my family, everyone participates and the steps are accomplished concurrently. For example, I combine Cleaning and Uncluttering and my husband simultaneously works on Repairing and Neutralizing. I keep a notepad with me to make Dynamizing notes while I'm working. By the time I've finished, I have become reacquainted with my house's features and selling points and have gained a clear vision of how Dynamizing will help communicate those features to a buyer. We review the Dynamizing plan and divide the chores to finish quickly and efficiently.

However, every house and every homeowner is different. Ideally, every homeseller would be given a ten-day grace period from home and career demands, could work uninterrupted through the program, and present the home in black-tie condition at the end of that time. I've never had an ideal situation. I've stretched the ten-day plan over a three-month period, and I've condensed it into as few as four days. The condition of your house and the time demands of your life will determine how quickly *your* plan can be accomplished. You may find your house needs more concentration on certain steps than others, or you may find that time is at a premium and you have only a few hours each day to focus on the program. Whichever is true for you, however, don't worry; the results will be just as spectacular whether you dress your house in a day or a month!

In a town house I prepared, very little Cleaning and Uncluttering were needed, and because of its size, painting was just a day's work. Dynamizing merely took a few hours of shopping and a few hours of staging. The entire program took four short, focused days from start to finish. Another time, however, I was preparing a huge home with lots of period detail. Because I was consulting on several projects, and due to the size of the house—eighteen rooms—as well as what I knew would be the expectations of the buyers looking in this price range, the program took six weeks with a team of three people working on various steps at various times. In my last house, due to life schedules and the lack of a moving deadline, we spread ten days over three months. At the opposite end: I have a client who was being transferred but hadn't watched the videotape until the day before the house was to be put on the market. After watching "Dress Your House For Success," they realized they could increase their house's appeal with Neutralizing and Dynamizing.

They stayed up all night and worked right up until the last minute before the Open House. It sold that day at full price!

Start by making a plan. (The checklists you'll find throughout this book will be helpful, too.) You may be inspired to start Dynamizing right away, but don't embark on this step until you complete the first four important steps of Uncluttering, Cleaning, Repairing, and Neutralizing. By sticking to these four basic steps, you'll be able to realize the full impact of Dynamizing.

Keep a master list in your notebook and make daily or individual lists to help plan work in smaller segments. Use a highlighter to cross things out. This helps you focus on how much you've accomplished rather than on how much you have left to accomplish. It's a small piece of advice that provides a big mental boost while you're involved in the work.

Write down exactly what you spend and keep receipts. At tax time, accurate records will mean you don't have to reconstruct your expenditures. You may want to ask a tax adviser about exactly what expenses can be deducted to know what you should keep track of. Be realistic about timing. If you don't have whole days available, break your plan into "after work" segments. For example, unclutter two rooms per night over a week, or clean on the weekend. Regardless of how much time you have, assign specific jobs to different family members. With everyone involved, the work becomes fun and the end result much more rewarding.

Make your plan fit your lifestyle.

In short, tailor the ten-day plan to fit your house and your life. It will be affected by time, condition of your house, and budget. Enlist the help of friends and relatives when you can; consolidate steps for efficiency; hire help for jobs that may take more time or know-how than you have; and allocate your budget where it will have the greatest impact.

You might be wondering how you can live in a house that is positioned, packaged, and staged to sell. It won't feel natural, and it shouldn't. A house packaged to sell has a completely different purpose than a house packaged for living. The good news is your house won't be on the market long.

Keep the end in view right from the start.

My Dress Your House for Success program is aimed at making the Open House a showstopping success—a show that closes on opening night.

Bear in mind the rewards of your work. You'll feel a real sense of satisfaction at what you've accomplished. Think, too, of the delighted reactions from buyers as they approach and tour your house, reactions that will translate into dollars.

There are no shortcuts or substitutions for these steps. Only one thing guarantees your house will take center stage: W-O-R-K. It's time to roll up your sleeves. If you're like me, you'll find that once you dig in, you'll enjoy the challenge of making your house irresistible.

4

STEP ONE: UNCLUTTERING

THE FIRST AND MOST important step to Dressing Your House for Success is Uncluttering.

Clutter is not only your everyday belongings; it encompassess decorating tastes as well. If you love the English country look of pillows stacked three deep and tabletops crowded with magazines, potpourri, candlesticks, and more, be aware that architectural structure and fine features become lost when clutter overtakes a house. A common problem with the collector look, for example— showcasing your precious collection of china teacups or decorative plates—is that

> **Clutter makes rooms and the entire house feel smaller. Who wants to buy smaller?**

impressive and interesting as it may be, people either become so engaged in the collection that they lose sight of your house or become so constricted by the claustrophobic feeling of too many things that they want to leave.

Consider the children's play space in your home: It may be a nice size, but if it's cluttered with toys, half-finished art projects, and worn-out furniture, it will feel cramped, messy, and overwhelming. Likewise, a kitchen with counters full of small appliances, handy gadgets, cookbooks, and cooking utensils will appear much smaller because it feels crowded.

If you can follow only one step in this book to the letter, this is the one. Uncluttering makes every room in your house look and feel more spacious, freeing up space both literally and in your buyer's mind.

When uncluttering, go through every room, every closet, every drawer, with the Uncluttering Rule uppermost in your mind: "When in doubt, throw it out . . . or sell it, store it, or give it away." Your goal: to create a roomy, comfortable feeling that's inviting to prospective buyers.

LIVING WITH BASICS ONLY

We can all live without much of the contents of our homes. Three houses ago, we found ourselves having temporarily to live in a rental. My house sold within hours of being put on the market and at full price, too, but one of the conditions was a quick closing. Not wanting to object to the conditions of such a great offer, we put most of our things in storage to avoid two major moves, keeping only the

Give your furniture and accessories a vacation.

basics: clothes for one season, a set of dishes, toiletries, and the most functional furniture. It was like packing for an extended vacation. If you're wondering whether to keep it out or store it, ask yourself if you're going to need it before your move.

A few years ago I prepared an eighteen-room Victorian house

for market. The owner had lived there for twenty years without letting go of any possessions, and in fact, the basement was full of things left from the previous owner. When a highly recommended Realtor refused to list the house, I was brought in as a specialist to prepare this house for sale.

Uncluttering can uncover a world of charm and space.

To unclutter this house, we rented a storage locker and hauled away a majority of the accumulated "treasures" before embarking on the rest of the program. The disarray of college memorabilia, file cabinets, desks, and countless office furnishings haphazardly left from when the house was used as office space, mountains of books, mismatched furnishings, rooms of children's toys, and more was overwhelming. Yet after removing this clutter, I opened up the possibility of returning the house to its original elegance. Within thirty days of completing step five, the house sold at nearly full price.

UNCLUTTERING AS ORGANIZING

Uncluttering is also organizing. Designate a specific "holding" place—such as a laundry basket—for items or parts you uncover that belong elsewhere. Be efficient and put away the odds and ends in one trip instead of running from room to room several times. By putting everything away neatly in place, your house relays the message that it has a perfect spot for everything. Buyers will *feel* that by living in your house, *they* could be well organized, too.

Show buyers a place for everything and everything in its place.

When to Combine Uncluttering and Cleaning

Some of the Uncluttering tasks really can't be separated from the Cleaning step. For example, to unclutter a drawer, first take absolutely everything out of that drawer. Some of the contents can be thrown or given away, while others will be put in your basket and returned to their rightful places. Before replacing the items, clean the drawer thoroughly. There's no reason to come back to this drawer in the Cleaning step. Once clean, add drawer organizers to hold small items in place, removing any chance that the cluttered look will return after a few drawer openings.

**Two steps
in one!**

Hidden Clutter—Closets

Closets are also apt to be cluttered. Unfortunately, closets are usually small spaces to begin with, so it's especially important to get rid of any clutter and carefully organize what remains. Throwing items unthinkingly into a closet and closing the door against the disarray that accumulates presents a problem—especially when cleaning for a house tour. Remember, potential buyers will want to inspect your closet space to see how much storage the house offers, and to imagine their possessions fitting into your closets. If the closets are already packed tight, buyers will feel that there just isn't room for them. But if closets look organized, buyers will begin to feel their life could also be organized in this house. Store items, if necessary, to create a more spacious feeling. (See the box on page 58 for more suggestions on preparing closets and drawers.)

Enhance by "Facing"

When Uncluttering, Cleaning, reorganizing, and returning items to a cupboard, cabinet, shelf, or closet, use a common merchandising technique called facing—displaying bottles, cans, and other items with the label facing forward. It generates a feeling of ease and organization. Next time you go to the grocery store, notice how meticulously the shelves are faced. Take advantage of this merchandising basic to enhance the orderliness and appeal of kitchen cupboards, medicine cabinets, bookshelves, closets, and more. Face everything from toiletries and spices to books and board games.

Manufacturers spend millions of dollars to achieve a certain look. You can have it for free.

When facing games and puzzles, stack them with the largest box on the bottom and the fronts flush to create an orderly look. If bookshelves are packed full, remove half of the books, preferably the worn-out paperbacks, creating a feeling of spaciousness.

Big Clutter—Furniture

Clutter is more than just the little stuff that accumulates, such as stacks of mail, the kids' art projects, etc. Too much furniture or too many accessories in a room also make it feel small and confining. If a piece of furniture

Less is more.

obstructs an expansive view of a room, move it so it doesn't block buyers' eyes from seeing the wonderful space in your home. When you can't find the right spot for a piece of furniture or an accessory, it belongs in storage.

DRAWERS, CLOSETS, CUPBOARDS, CABINETS, BUILT-INS

Remove everything.

Consolidate. Sort through and keep what will be needed before the move. Consolidate containers of the same products (duplicate supplies and food). If necessary, remove a few items; cupboards are most attractive when they look well "stocked," not crammed. Closets look the most appealing when there is space to add more, not when they're jammed to capacity.

Clean or paint. If it's a closet, paint the interior; if it's not, scrub it thoroughly. If you replace shelf liner, use white (avoid self-adhesive—it's time-consuming and more expensive). Use a gentle abrasive cleanser to remove stubborn stains.

It only takes a few minutes to paint a closet. Wrap paintbrushes in plastic wrap or use disposable brushes rather than cleaning up each time and you'll find you're more likely to paint each closet and do the little touch-ups that transform an ordinary closet or cupboard into a distinctive feature.

Clean, replace, and face all items.

❑ Wipe down containers with a glass cleaner and face each one as you replace it — labels to the front, grouped by size.

❑ Group like items together and use organizers or small plastic containers for smaller items that will shift and look cluttered after a few drawer openings. Purchase clear closet storage boxes to present an image of order.

❑ Tri-fold linens for a stylized look, making sure no raw edges show.

❑ Use the same kind and color of hangers in all clothes closets. Hang all clothes like a department store display: in groups and facing the same direction. Add shoe or boot racks.

Remove as much clutter and excess furniture as possible, stopping just short of stark. While it's important to remove any excess to showcase your space, a stark room or minimally outfitted room projects an empty feeling that nothing happens here. Empty houses do not sell more quickly or profitably. Lifelessness is not only a difficult negative to overcome, it also attracts low offers because it sends the message that it *must sell;* the owners have moved on and need to unload their house. If you have to move before your house sells, rent furniture so it still looks inhabited.

> **Empty says desperate to sell and hides the life of a house.**

Plant Clutter

Houseplants are a great decorating tool because they add life and fill empty space. But beware. A lot of plants or unhealthy ones —especially cuttings or those you're attempting to revive—are clutter. Remove them while your house is on the market.

I was asked by a friend to look at a house he was considering purchasing. The house was gorgeous: Curb appeal was strong. The entryway was open and inviting, and the living room . . . well, it may have been lovely. I don't remember. My eyes immediately focused on a decrepit-looking tree with only five wilted leaves on it right in the middle of a beautiful bay window. The owner saw my shocked expression and explained that she was nursing it back to life. To this day, I describe that

> **Houseplants make a memorable statement. Be sure it's positive.**

house as the one with the half-dead tree. Don't give buyers this kind of opportunity to recall your house in a negative way.

Too Many Doors Are Clutter

Doors that stand open most of the time—at the end of hallways or at entrances to kitchens, dining rooms, even basements—can make a room feel smaller or block a great view just because of the sheer mass of the door. While we don't normally think of doors as clutter, they can make an area feel much smaller and tighter than is necessary. If you don't use a door, take it off its hinges and store it in the garage. The new owner can decide whether he wants to put it back. We took off a door to our kitchen because when it was open (as it usually was), it blocked an entire wall in a tight hallway. Once it was removed, we used that wall to hang artwork. Instead of being blocked by a door, the wall with the newly hung artwork made the entrance to the kitchen feel larger and more open.

Open doors create a closed feeling.

Sell It, Store It, or Give It Away

As you unclutter, box up excess or outdated items for donation to a charitable organization such as the Goodwill or Salvation Army. Consignment shops are an alternative for everything from sporting goods and clothing to extra furniture. Many charitable groups, however, actively search for clothing, furniture, and

Recycling is good for the environment and good for the soul.

MOVING WITH KIDS

Make a special effort to include your children in all stages of the move. Since their world centers around home and friends, your changing those safe environments can be difficult and scary for them. Ask for their suggestions and encourage them to share their ideas. Being involved permits kids to talk about their feelings, helping them adjust better to the move. Turn moving into an adventure and ease the transition to a new home.

✔ Talk to children early on about the reasons for the move. Prepare them by taking photos of the new house, their room, neighborhood, and school.

✔ Listen to their feelings and watch for signs of stress. Children will look to you for cues on how to cope. When the stress of selling begins to take its toll, step back and relax. You'll be a better role model.

✔ Give your children a "memory box." Any sturdy box will do. Then help them sort important items to save (school awards, a favorite drawing, notes from friends, etc.). Explain that the boxes will be carefully stored in your new home. Memory boxes provide a link to days gone by and rekindle sweet memories no matter how often you move.

✔ Include your children in every step of your selling plan. Let them know how important their role is.

✔ Don't expect perfection. When you see signs of stress or regressive behavior, take time—now. It can help avoid bigger issues down the road.

other everyday items, and you'll be helping others while also helping yourself. Not only are you eligible for a tax deduction, you save the time involved in organizing a garage sale. If, however, you decide to hold a sale, do it now or store your inventory until the house is sold. Having a successful garage sale is easy but requires preparation. I've never had a garage sale that didn't make a *lot of money*. (See page 176 for tips on how to throw a financially successful garage sale.)

Uncluttering costs absolutely nothing. In fact, if you sell the myriad possessions you unearth while Uncluttering, you can actually *make* money, which is useful in the next four steps.

UNCLUTTERING AS THERAPY

A word to the heart. Uncluttering can be therapeutic—renewing a link to the past. Be prepared for attacks of nostalgia as you uncover old letters, photographs, and more. I have specific boxes filled with memorabilia that I rarely open. I never throw them out, but can't resist going through them when I'm Uncluttering for a move.

The last time I moved, I came across an "I love you" note that my now-grown son had written to Santa and another he had written to me telling me he had broken one of my favorite vases. I laughed and cried. Take time for these kinds of feelings. It's a normal part of letting a house go, while taking the memories with you.

Take time for gentle reminders of days gone by.

While I'm never quite prepared for the nostalgia, I am even less prepared for the initial chaos of this step. Don't panic when you look around and see the contents of every drawer emptied out, the closet contents spread out all over the floor, and the laundry basket filling up with items waiting to go elsewhere. Order will reign again.

UNCLUTTERING MAKES FOR A SMOOTH MOVE

A bonus of Uncluttering is that it will make your upcoming move smoother. With everything in its place and no "extras" to ponder as you pack, the actual move will be quick and easy. We packed our last house—twelve rooms—in a matter of days. Because packing was so organized, Uncluttering made unpacking in our new house a snap, too.

USING THE CHECKLISTS

When you're ready to begin, use this checklist (and those at the ends of Chapters 5, 6, 7, and 8) and add your own "to do" items to develop personal, customized lists. In my household we act like a SWAT team and schedule the steps on a calendar to involve every household member. Set goals and the rewards for meeting them—rent a movie, go out for pizza.

UNCLUTTERING, INSIDE AND OUT

Exterior/Curb Appeal

❑ Clear the street in front of your house of any litter or debris so it looks impeccably clean from the corner right up to your front door.

❑ Pick up and carefully organize tools and gardening equipment. Coil hoses neatly.

❑ Thoroughly weed garden and shrub areas. Remove fallen sticks and leaves.

❑ Give your lawn a fresh mowing so it looks healthy, cared for, and well groomed. Resod any bare spots as needed.

❑ Trim plants and shrubs to create a feeling of orderliness and precision.

❑ Remove and replace any dead or dying shrubs.

❑ Clear away bikes, toys, and extra cars from the driveway. If you have a fix-it hobbyist in the house who has spare parts everywhere, show no mercy—find someplace else for working on cars, bikes, boats, etc.

❑ _____

❑ _____

❑ _____

Entryway

- ❏ Closets:

  - • Remove, consolidate, clean or paint, face all coats and jackets on wood hangers.

  - • Remove shoes, boots, sporting equipment, etc.

- ❏ If your hall table is a mail collection spot, clear it off and select an alternative location or place mail in an attractive wood box or basket.

- ❏ If you're selling a condominium or apartment, make certain that other occupants' mail and deliveries are picked up daily. Consider talking to each occupant and let them know you are willing to be on "entryway duty" during the time your unit is on the market.

- ❏ _____

- ❏ _____

- ❏ _____

Kitchen

This is the heart of your home, and many buyers feel it is the most important room in the house. Your efforts here can have a major impact on the sale price.

- ❏ Counters: Clear them off. Store small appliances, gadgets, pots, pans, and bowls.

❑ Cupboards, drawers, and cabinets:

- Remove, consolidate, clean or paint interior, clean and face contents.

- Group like items together (baking pans, serving pieces, etc.) to create a feeling of space and ease. Purchase organizers to make efficient use of tight space.

- Silverware drawers. Purchase a new organizer if yours is worn. Sort the drawer so all similar utensils are together.

- Cooking-utensil drawers. They don't need to look like a junk drawer. Sort through your spatulas, wooden spoons, etc., and store what you don't need. Use dividers and organizers.

- Everyone has a junk drawer, and probably everyone needs one. This is an opportunity to show potential buyers how "perfect" your home is. Purchase drawer organizers or use small food containers to create an organized look. (There is a "junk drawer organizer" on the market.) Place all tape, pencils, and scissors together; screwdrivers and measuring tape together, etc.

❑ Refrigerator:

- Remove and consolidate extra items.

- Take out the shelves and wash and shine with glass cleaner. Wipe off food containers and consolidate. Face the items as you replace each one.

- Add a box of baking soda to remove odors and ensure a fresh, clean smell.

❑ Under the sink:

- Remove, consolidate, clean or paint interior, clean and face all items.

- Add a paper-bag holder or door organizer to hold items and get them off the floor.

- Throw out dirty rags.

- Scrub the flooring. If it is stained, paint or add a linoleum remnant.

- Put cleaning products and containers into a pail or holder.

❑ Plants: Give away or discard unhealthy plants. Cuttings, too.

❑ Memo areas: Remove papers and notes, children's artwork, chipped or broken magnets.

❑ _____

❑ _____

❑ _____

Bathrooms

❑ Counters: Clear them off and store all personal-care products out of sight.

❑ Vanities, medicine cabinets, linen closets:

  • Remove, consolidate, clean or paint interior, clean and face all items.

  • Put makeup into a basket or case.

  • Group cleaning supplies in a bucket.

  • If your shelves are old and stained or sticky from too many years of self-adhesive paper, consider painting or replacing them with new glass shelves.

❑ _____

❑ _____

Bedrooms

❑ Drawers, closets, built-ins: Remove, consolidate, clean or paint, clean and face articles and clothing.

❑ Remove extra furniture to create space.

❑ Sort through children's play areas. Box extra toys and recycle or sell old ones.

❑ _____

❑ _____

Living Room/Dining Room/Family Room

❑ Remove all papers and magazines from coffee and end tables.

❑ Rearrange furniture for openness. Remove and store, sell, or give away excess.

❑ Remove unhealthy and extra plants. Take down hanging plants. They block the light and get in the way of buyers seeing a room. Plants are more pleasing when you look down at them instead of up at the bottom of a pot.

❑ Weed out excess books from bookcases.

❑ _____

❑ _____

❑ _____

Basement/Garage/Attic

These are major storage areas and can seem overwhelming if you have accumulated years of mementos, souvenirs, and other paraphernalia. Take on one room at a time. You'll feel a real sense of accomplishment and be much more enthusiastic about completing the job when you can see the difference your efforts have made. A good rule of thumb is, if it's in storage, you won't need it until you move, so box and move it off the property or sell it if you no longer use it.

❑ Garage, tool, and storage rooms:

- Sort, box, and store tools, shop equipment, and projects.

- Hang tools, sports equipment, and lawn and garden equipment on the wall with organizers.

- Store paint cans on shelves. If you don't have shelves, purchase inexpensive sturdy shelving. Move it to your new house to start out organized.

❑ Laundry room:

- Sort and straighten laundry area.

- Group and face soap, stain removers, fabric softeners.

- Take worn-out and outgrown clothes to a charity or consignment store.

❑ Attic: Box and store, sell, or give away everything in the attic. Neatly stacked boxes are acceptable, but be certain they don't block a buyer's view of the storage space.

❑ If you have an amusement room or play area in the basement, sort, box, and store toys and games.

❑ _____

❑ _____

Backyard/Deck/Balcony

- ❏ Pick up all toys, gardening tools, and equipment.

- ❏ Remove and store any building or repairing projects in progress.

- ❏ Remove excess railing decorations and pots from balconies.

- ❏ Remove all but a few furnishings from balconies to convey spaciousness.

- ❏ _____

- ❏ _____

5

Step Two: Cleaning

THE EVERYDAY CLEANING of once over lightly with a dust rag and vacuum that most of us do might be just fine for family and friends. When you want to sell your house for top dollar, just fine isn't good enough.

A buyer going through your home might like the downstairs and start her way upstairs. The master bedroom really sparks her interest, and as she thinks seriously about your house, she begins to look more carefully. Entering the master bath, she pulls back the shower curtain and comes to a halt.

The shower floor is covered with a layer of soap scum and the grout is mildewed. Now, this particular buyer may have trouble looking much further. Even if she moves past that dirty bathroom, she'll feel uncomfortable, a little embarrassed, and even tentative about opening doors. She mentally disengages because she's slightly afraid of what else she might find. For the rest of the tour, she will be remote, somewhat hesitant, and will regard

> **The uncomfortable feeling of an unclean house causes apprehension, and the buyer will start to disengage.**

your house with a disinterested attitude. And guaranteed, she will remember that filthy master bathroom—if she thinks of your house at all.

Clean every inch of space and every item in it. A deeply clean house not only looks great, it *feels* uplifting and as new as when you first bought it. Buyers will be eager to explore every nook and cranny in an immaculate house and will sense that the house has been cared for lovingly.

Conceive of this step as spring cleaning to the nth degree, where you dig in and attack everything: dust, dirt, furniture, fingerprints—even odors. No fixture should go untouched, from the basement plumbing pipes up to the attic beams. Pay special attention to kitchens, bathrooms, nurseries, and pet areas.

A whole new kind of clean.

Although giving the house a thorough cleaning is not a difficult chore, forgetting to clean one little area is easy. For example, I failed to notice the miniblinds in my bathroom had a layer of dust and accumulated dirt that made them look old and dingy. An alert buyer would notice the accumulation of dirt right away and feel that my house hadn't been properly maintained. After I washed the blinds, the entire bathroom had a different—lighter, brighter, and more inviting—feeling!

If you have a pet, have it meticulously groomed to avoid offending potential buyers. I'll never forget touring a house we were quite serious about purchasing. We had driven by it several times. It was in a great neighborhood, the price was right, and the features exactly matched our checklist. We were so excited about the house that we arrived early for our appointment. The owners had already moved out so we peeked in the windows. It looked fabulous! We could hardly wait for the agent to arrive.

When he did, we started on the first floor and loved what we saw. My husband went upstairs and called down for me to come and see the great master bedroom. Acci-

Pet owner's alert.

dentally, I turned down the hall the other way and was met by such an overpoweringly strong animal smell that I gagged. I joined my husband and quickly finished the tour, nervous about what else I'd uncover. I couldn't imagine how I would ever rid the house of that repulsive smell. As a result, we didn't buy that house.

Homes with smokers require extra cleaning and extra attention to odors. Smoke settles on everything in a house: windows, plants, clothing, and bric-a-brac. Use a carpet freshener each time you vacuum to maintain a fresh scent, and consider smoking outside while your house is on the market.

HOW MUCH DOES IT COST TO CLEAN?

Cleaning supplies cost approximately $25 to $50, more if you rent equipment such as a rug shampooer or a floor polisher. If, however, you're pressed for time or just aren't a thorough cleaner yourself, hire professional cleaners to help with this step.

An experienced house cleaner can cost $65 or more per day

GETTING STARTED

Assemble two totes or baskets (gardening totes are ideal) and a painting kit. Leave one tote empty; you'll use it to collect out-of-place items you find throughout the house that need to be returned to their proper place. In the other, collect all your cleaning supplies:

- ❏ small bucket
- ❏ paper towels
- ❏ sponges
- ❏ glass cleaner
- ❏ cleanser
- ❏ scratch cover
- ❏ rust remover

- ❏ screwdrivers
- ❏ single-edge razor—for paint drops and glue residue
- ❏ notepad and pencil
- ❏ hand vac
- ❏ plastic garbage bags

YOUR PAINT KIT WILL CONTAIN

- ❏ flat white latex paint
- ❏ drop cloths (disposable or cloth)
- ❏ masking tape and edgers

- ❏ paint brushes and rollers (reusable or disposable)
- ❏ plastic wrap
- ❏ paint stirrers

depending on your area. Skilled help with heavy cleaning, window washing, and more can cost $10 to $20 per hour. If pets or smokers are part of your household, have your carpets professionally cleaned. Plan to spend approximately $100 to $200 for a whole-house carpet-cleaning package. Bear in mind that every dollar invested in hired help buys you time to attend to other aspects of the process.

CLEAN AND POLISH ALL WOODWORK

W alk through your house and carefully examine every piece of wood and paneling. Woodwork gets tired looking and worn, and yet this daily wear and tear doesn't show up as easily on wood as it does on painted surfaces. Rather than look dirty, the wood gradually becomes dull looking. By cleaning and restoring woodwork, you enhance your house with a warm glow.

The recreation room in my last house had knotty-pine paneling that had become dingy. My teenage son was the only person who used the room, so none of us noticed that the paneling was dull and lifeless. When it came time to sell, however, I wanted to open up the possibilities of that room to include a home-office space, a cheerful playroom for small children, and more. So I looked carefully at every aspect of the room and saw that the paneling was in

Cast a glow on your house.

worse shape than I had thought, with many small nail holes and tape residue from posters my teenager had hung. It needed cleaning badly. I began by using a wood soap and then went over the entire room with a scratch cover. What a miracle! It covered up scratches and chips, deepened the color of the wood, and made the whole room glow.

CLEAN WINDOWS LET THE LIGHT SHINE IN

N atural light adds warmth to a house in a way nothing else can. Clean windows play a key role in creating a bright feeling. They must be sparkling inside and out.

CLEANING BASICS

WINDOWS

☐ Clean to a sparkle, inside and out. Pay special attention to the sills between the window and the wall.

☐ Hire a professional if you don't have time to do a thorough job.

CURTAINS AND DRAPES

☐ Dry-clean and launder.

☐ If curtains are old and faded, consider miniblinds for a current and spacious look.

FLOORING

☐ Wash and wax linoleum and wood floors. Polish to a shine.

☐ Clean and deodorize carpeting.

WOODWORK AND DOORS

☐ Clean or polish.

☐ Touch up with paint or scratch cover.

☐ Repaint or refinish where needed.

Sunlight pouring in through a window and highlighting the shiny clean finish on a wood table or floor can't possibly happen with streaked or dirty windows. Don't forget skylights, too. A newly cleaned skylight lit up our whole bathroom. It hadn't even appeared dirty, but after cleaning it, we discovered how much the rain and dust had dimmed its positive effect. Pay close attention to other glass surfaces such as picture frames, mirrors, and artwork. Clean them carefully so their reflective surfaces sparkle and shine.

Pay special attention to light—both natural and artificial—as you work through the steps. Lighting is an important part of any show, and real estate professionals find that buyers respond much more favorably to houses flooded with sunlight. A well-lit house is warm, inviting, and pleasing to the senses. Carefully examine your windows and remove any plants or knick-knacks that clutter the sills and block the sun. Take notes as to where the sunlight falls at various times of day. These bright, sunny areas contribute to staging positive, lasting impressions.

Let the sunshine light up your stage.

To make clean surfaces sparkle even more, maximize both natural and artificial light. Clean all the lightbulbs throughout your house. Dust accumulates quickly, making the light they throw off diffused and dull. Consider replacing the bulbs with new ones for the brightest light possible.

IF IT CAN'T BE CLEANED, PAINT IT!

If you can't clean it, my rule of thumb is to paint it. A coat of fresh paint invites a new beginning. Most people marvel at the way their house looks after completing this step. The response I hear most often is, "My house looks and feels like new!"

CLEANING, INSIDE AND OUT

Exterior/Curb Appeal

❑ Sidewalk and walkway:

  • Sweep completely clean.

  • Remove any weeds or grass that have grown up between the cracks.

  • Hose down sidewalks and walkways for a thoroughly clean, inviting look.

  • In winter, use sand or salt on ice patches; shovel snow, leaving neat, tidy edges on pathways.

❑ Fastidiously dispose of any and all pet debris.

❑ Driveway: Clean up oil and other stains.

❑ Siding: Wash for a fresh, bright look and feel. Professional services are available with products especially designed to restore vinyl and aluminum siding.

❑ Windows: Use glass cleaner on the inside and outside to ensure a bright, clean sparkle. The garage windows and skylights, too.

❑ Gutters: Clean out all debris.

❑ Eaves: Hose down.

❑ _____

Entryway

- ❑ Windows: Clean to a sparkle.

- ❑ Walls and ceilings: Paint or clean.

- ❑ Curtains and drapes: Launder. Replace if needed.

- ❑ Floors: Scrub and polish to a shine.

- ❑ Woodwork and doors: Clean and polish.

- ❑ Polish doorknobs and light fixtures.

- ❑ _____

- ❑ _____

Kitchen

A clean-looking and clean-smelling kitchen is essential. Use lemon-scented products to prolong the clean scent.

- ❑ Cupboards and drawers:

  - Wipe down the insides making sure all surfaces are squeaky, sparkling clean. Use a soft cleanser on laminate shelves.

  - Use a glass cleaner on the outside of laminate cupboards.

  - Use a wood soap on wood cabinets and then a scratch cover, which can be a transformation wonder, available for both light and dark woods.

- Small appliances: Wipe them down before storing. The blender with food splatters will draw negative attention when a pantry or cupboard is opened, but a sparkling clean blender will convey a well-cared-for, like-new feeling.

- Refrigerator: Wipe down outside. Don't forget the top!

- Stove:

  - Clean the oven to a sparkle.

  - Use a single-edge razor to clean baked-on grease off a door and then shine with a glass cleaner.

  - Replace the oven lightbulb.

  - Clean or replace burner liners.

- Vents and exhaust hoods: Clean and deodorize.

- Sinks:

  - Polish and clean.

  - Remove stains and mineral buildup around faucets.

  - Clean the tile grout. Use a grout cleaner or recaulk.

  - Run a lemon section through the garbage disposal for a fresh smell.

- Windows: Clean to a sparkle.

- ❑ Walls and ceilings: Clean all cooking residue.

- ❑ Curtains and drapes: Launder, replace if needed.

- ❑ Light fixtures, track lighting:

  - • Wipe off lightbulbs.

  - • Wash out fixtures or vacuum inside of track lighting.

- ❑ Flooring: Wash and wax to a brilliant glow. Remove old wax if your floors are yellowed.

- ❑ Woodwork and doors: Wipe down, polish, use scratch cover.

- ❑ _____

- ❑ _____

Bathrooms

- ❑ Windows: Clean to a sparkle.

- ❑ Walls and ceilings: Wipe down to remove water spots.

- ❑ Curtains and drapes: Launder. Replace if needed.

- ❑ Flooring: Scrub and wax.

- ❑ Woodwork and doors: Clean and polish.

- ❑ Smells: Use lemon cleaning products.

- ❏ Polish all chrome to a sparkle. Don't forget the pipes underneath the sink, even if they are in a vanity!

- ❏ Remove all rust stains from sink, toilet, tub, and shower.

- ❏ Remove mineral buildup around faucets.

- ❏ Remove all mildew from tub and shower area.

- ❏ Clean all grout thoroughly. Use a grout whitener and recaulk where needed.

- ❏ Scrub tile until it shines. Finish with glass cleaner.

- ❏ Wash the shower curtain. If it doesn't look like new, replace it.

- ❏ Clean shower doors thoroughly. Remove soap residue and shine.

- ❏ Add toilet bowl cleaner and sanitizer. Keep the lid down.

- ❏ _____

- ❏ _____

Bedrooms

- ❏ Launder or dry-clean comforters and bedspreads.

- ❏ Windows: Clean to a sparkle.

- ❑ Curtains and drapes: Launder. Replace if needed.

- ❑ Flooring: Wash wood floors, clean carpets.

- ❑ Woodwork and doors: Clean and polish.

- ❑ Wash and clean lighting fixtures and lamps.

- ❑ _____

- ❑ _____

Living Room/Dining Room/Family Room

- ❑ Windows: Clean to a sparkle.

- ❑ Walls and ceilings: Paint a fresh, clean white.

- ❑ Drapes: Dry-clean or launder. Add blinds if worn and dated.

- ❑ Use a wood oil and polish your furniture, woodwork, and wood floors to a glow.

- ❑ Clean and deodorize carpeting and rugs.

- ❑ Clean and polish all lighting fixtures to a sparkle.

- ❑ Clean inside and outside of fireplaces. Polish fireplace tools to a glow.

- ❑ _____

- ❑ _____

Basement/Attic/Garage

❑ Vacuum basement floors and ceilings. If you have more than dust on your ceilings (cobwebs) or see any signs of insects or rodents, call an exterminator. No buyer will feel comfortable being greeted by basement pests no matter how harmless.

❑ Vacuum attic floors. In one house, I scrubbed the painted wood floors and it made a major difference. Instead of old and dark, it felt fresh and spacious.

❑ Sweep garage floors, clean grease.

❑ Don't forget the garage and basement windows. Let the sunlight brighten these areas.

❑ Thoroughly clean and deodorize all pet areas.

❑ Wipe down all appliances: washer, dryer, water heater, water softener, furnace. Every interested buyer will look at them. Clean and shiny will say they are in good order.

❑ If you have wood paneling, polish and restore it.

❑ _____

❑ _____

Backyard/Deck/Balcony

❑ Clean the deck and use a sealer to make it look like new. (After performing this step on one of my own houses, the appraiser asked if our fifteen-year-old deck was built recently!)

❑ Wipe down all lawn furniture, grills, and pool or spa equipment.

❑ Hose down screens in gazebos or porches.

❑ Wipe down railings on balconies.

❑ _____

❑ _____

6

STEP THREE: REPAIRING

WITH THE CLUTTER gone and every area sparkling clean, concentrate on repairs. It may surprise you how many little things now stand out, requiring attention.

A house cannot sell for top dollar if any detail, large or small, is in less than perfect shape. Even small maintenance needs such as a leaky faucet in the basement, a cracked bathroom tile, or peeling paint on one side of the house send out a warning signal to buyers—work, work, work, which costs money, money, money. These warning signals trigger a fear response—fear that larger problems are lurking beneath the surface. Everyone knows that if a house receives poor or insufficient maintenance, serious problems can quickly arise.

Repairs mean work. And work means time. We all have enough work and not enough time.

Buyers perceive household repairs, large or small, as taking time away from what they enjoy doing. Repairs also cost money —money they could spend in much more exciting ways.

Neglect repairs and you position your house as a fixer upper, significantly decreasing both the number of potential buyers and the price they'll pay. When a house is in need of repairs, buyers will feel justified in making low offers since they're likely calculating an inflated repair cost in their offer. No one wants to spend their own time, money, and effort on something that should have been fixed in the first place. As a homeseller, do not underestimate the importance of repairing absolutely everything, no matter how small, from a leak in the roof to a cracked switchplate. Anyone interested in the house should not receive even the slightest inkling that she'll have to put any work into it. Chances are if you think something is too much trouble to fix, buyers will think so, too.

> **You position your house as a "fixer upper" when you put it on the market in need of repair.**

If you don't have the time or desire to make necessary repairs, save everyone a lot of trouble by lowering the price to reflect the state of your house. Or, take care of repairs, make your house look like new, and pocket the return on your investment in the form of a great offer. Repairing isn't remodeling. Major improvements—such as kitchens, bathrooms, additions, even fireplaces—are not what you want to undertake when selling a house. They seldom result in a dollar-for-dollar return, and if such improvements are called for, buyers would probably rather pay a lower price and remodel themselves to their tastes. The price reduction could be the same as or less than the expense of remodeling. If your kitchen cabinets look dull and dated, a fresh coat of paint and shiny new hardware will make them look attractive and new at a fraction of the cost of new cabinetry.

MAKE A COMPLETE LIST OF REPAIRS, SMALL AND LARGE

Go through your house with your notepad and the checklists from this book and decide what you'll need to repair. Write down everything, from larger jobs such as repairing front steps and regrouting the shower stall to smaller items like leaky faucets and ripped screens. Pay attention to all the little details, because each one contrib utes to the big picture. For example, it's easy to see a broken piece of woodwork that needs attention, but mismatched switchplates are not as noticeable. In a model home, the switchplates would all match. If you have a combination of white, off-white, and brown switchplates or outlet covers, you're sending a subtle message of imperfection.

With buyer's eyes you'll see every repair that needs attention.

While making a list of repairs, ask yourself, "Does it look like new?" Watch out for the tendency to say, "Oh, it's not really that bad," because that usually means the opposite is true. Repair it, paint it, or replace it so it looks like new.

When we went through our last house making the repair list, we included the birdhouse poles in our backyard. In this house, the backyard was a major selling point, with mature landscaping and perennial gardens, a tiled swimming pool, a cedar deck, and a gazebo. It also had four birdhouses, two of which were on poles that had badly stained over the years. Over time, we had gotten used to the way these poles looked. It was a detail we almost classified as "good enough," but at the last minute my husband scraped and painted these two poles. Sure enough, at the Open House, a buyer exclaimed, "What a fabulous house—everything is in such good condition—even the birdhouses look new."

HOW MUCH WILL REPAIRS COST?

Repair costs are entirely dependent on the condition of your house. In general, basic maintenance expenses are a low-cost/high-gain proposition. For example, fixing a dripping faucet may be as easy as buying a new washer at twenty-five cents. However, a buyer may equate that dripping faucet with faulty plumbing and translate it into thousands of dollars—or a low offer on your house. In this case, your twenty-five-cent investment will reap huge financial benefits.

Buyers won't pay top dollar for a house with a leaky roof, malfunctioning furnace, or faulty plumbing. While these major repairs are necessary to put your house at the top of the price range, don't expect to recoup all the replacement costs. You won't have to settle for a lower offer than if you didn't contract for those repairs, but every house needs a roof, a furnace, and plumbing, and buyers will expect—but not necessarily pay for—them to be in good condition.

Top dollar demands top repair, from the roof to the plumbing.

Don't let major repairs stand between you and the offer you want. You can offer a repair allowance, but chances are if you go ahead and make the repairs yourself, it will cost less than what you'd have to reduce your price by. Keep in mind that most buyers are looking for move-in condition, and having to make immediate, especially large, repairs will be seen as a negative, no matter who pays for them.

As an example of costs, following is what I spent on repairs while preparing the last house I sold:

Reseal grout in master shower (hired help)	$90.00
Miscellaneous outlet replacements, switchplates, laundry-tub backflow, basement drain covers, conduit	40.00
Tighten doorknobs	-0-
Replace gate latch	25.00
Front stairs:	135.00
Repair crumbling concrete (hired help)	
Use a concrete sealer	
Replace garage door bottom seal	15.00
Fill space between brick and siding that had separated over the years (hired help)	85.00
Dig up and relay patio blocks (hired help)	80.00
Clean out and fill gap between driveway and garage (hired help)	75.00
Replace patio screen door	50.00
Clean and treat deck	35.00
Total repair costs	**$630.00**

REPAIR AND DISCLOSE

A word of caution: Don't try to hide or cover up problem areas. Homeowners are obligated by law to disclose any known defects, and most cities require an inspection certificate before you can put your house on the market. Buyers will often include an inspection as a contingency in their offer. They'll hire professional home inspectors to analyze a house including its roof, mechanical systems, interior and exterior condition, and any appliances that remain. Inspectors look for both existing and potential problems, so repairing flaws now will save time and stress after you receive an offer.

Consider investing in a seller's inspection—hiring a home-inspection company or engineer. The report will inform you of problems you might not see, and you can-deal with them before they appear on the buyer's inspection report. You may be able to include the cost of an inspection in your selling price, and if you share the report with buyers, it will build confidence about the condition of your house. In addition, some home-sellers purchase a home warranty plan, which guarantees a defect-free house for a specific period of time. In a competitive market, this could set you apart.

A professional home inspector sees even deeper than buyer's eyes.

REPAIRING BASICS

WINDOWS

❏ Replace any cracked or broken panes.

❏ Repair any wood rot.

❏ Recaulk where needed.

❏ Make sure every window opens easily, and that all shades, blinds, and shutters are in proper working condition.

WALLS AND CEILINGS

❏ Patch all cracks and nail holes.

FLOORING

❏ Replace missing or loose tiles.

❏ Glue any loose seams in linoleum. Replace if worn.

❏ If carpet can't be cleaned or is threadbare, replace it or take it up and finish wood floors.

WOODWORK AND DOORS

❏ Fill cracks and nail holes. Stain or paint to match.

❏ Tighten loose doorknobs and cabinet pulls.

❏ Lubricate squeaky hinges.

Exterior/Curb Appeal

❏ Fence: Make sure gates—hinges and catches—work easily and noiselessly. A squeaky gate or a broken fence spells work for a buyer. If a fence is dull looking, add a fresh coat of paint or stain. It will enhance the appeal of your entire house.

❏ Walkways and steps: Repair cracks and any broken or crumbling steps. These are not only dangerous; they detract from your home's overall charm.

❏ Foundation: Repair any cracks immediately. A strong, secure foundation is critical to a home's fundamental appeal.

❏ The roof: Carefully evaluate the condition of your roof. Consider having a new roof put on if your home is in dire need of one. The roof is always a major concern.

  • Replace broken or missing roof shingles.

  • Repair flashings.

❏ Gutters and downspouts: Repair or replace if necessary. Neat gutters dress up a home's exterior.

❏ Driveway: Repair cracks, crumblings, or separations from the house. Driveway patch and sealer is easy to work with and the results give a finished look and a cared-for feel.

❏ Windows:

- Replace cracked or broken glass.

- Repair any wood rot.

- Recaulk where needed.

- Repair or replace any screens that look brittle, pushed out, or anything less than taut.

- Touch up with paint wherever needed.

❏ Doors:

- Tighten doorknobs.

- Oil squeaky hinges to usher buyers gracefully and quietly into the house.

- Replace rollers in sliding doors if they stick or jam. New rollers are inexpensive, easy to install, and make for smooth sliding.

❏ Doorbells: Ensure that doorbells work. All children will try them, and it will definitely draw attention if they don't chime!

❏ Look at every detail. Even a basketball hoop with a torn net will be noticed by a buyer.

❏ _____

❏ _____

❏ _____

Entryway

- ❑ Windows: Repair as needed.

- ❑ Doors: Tighten doorknobs; oil squeaky hinges.

- ❑ Thresholds must be secure. Replace rotted or cracked wood.

- ❑ Replace and match any broken switchplates or outlet covers.

- ❑ _____

- ❑ _____

Kitchen

- ❑ Cupboards and drawers: Check all hinges and knobs. Tighten loose knobs, replace broken hardware.

- ❑ Counters: Repair or replace chipped countertops or tile.

- ❑ Appliances: Check lights and timers. Repair as needed.

- ❑ Sinks: Repair leaky faucets. Check pipes underneath sink.

- ❑ Windows: Repair as needed. Make sure shades, blinds, and shutters work effortlessly.

- ❑ Floors: If your floor is badly worn, adding new neutral flooring or tile will be an added attraction to buyers.

- ❑ Walls and ceilings: Patch and repair as needed.

- ❑ Light fixtures: Fix or replace if dull and dated looking.

- ❑ Replace and match any broken switchplates or outlet covers.

- ❑ _____

- ❑ _____

- ❑ _____

Bathroom

- ❑ Windows: Recaulk as needed. Make sure blinds are working.

- ❑ Walls and ceiling: Patch and repair as needed.

- ❑ Make any needed repairs to toilets and plumbing.

- ❑ Patch, repair, or replace grout and caulking.

- ❑ Replace any cracked or missing tiles.

- ❑ Replace old or cracked toilet seat or cover.

- ❑ Replace and match any broken switchplates or outlet covers.

- ❑ _____

- ❑ _____

Bedrooms

- ❏ Windows: Repair as needed.

- ❏ Walls and ceilings: Patch and repair as needed.

- ❏ Replace and match any broken switchplates or outlet covers.

- ❏ _____

- ❏ _____

Living Room/Dining Room/Family Room

- ❏ Windows: Repair as needed.

- ❏ Walls and ceilings: Patch and repair as needed.

- ❏ Flooring: Repair squeaky floors, replace carpeting if necessary.

- ❏ Replace and match any broken switchplates or outlet covers.

- ❏ _____

- ❏ _____

Basement/Attic/Garage

- ❏ Make certain all appliances are in working order. Have a technician inspect and certify the condition.

❑ Make certain all pipes, laundry connections, and exhaust pipes are in good working order. Repair if needed.

❑ Windows: Repair as needed.

❑ Walls and ceilings: Repair as needed. If you have corrected water damage or other damage, make sure no sign remains. It's important not to hide any currently damaged area. Fix it.

❑ Replace and match any broken switchplates or outlet covers.

❑ _____

❑ _____

Backyard/Deck/Balcony

❑ Nail down any loose boards on deck.

❑ Repair screens on outdoor porches.

❑ Repair or replace broken tiles in a pool or spa.

❑ Make sure all pool and spa equipment is in working condition: filter, heater.

❑ Tighten railings. Touch up chipped or rusted areas with paint or stain.

❑ _____

❑ _____

7

STEP FOUR: NEUTRALIZING

CREATING A NEUTRAL environment that accommodates virtually anyone's furnishings finalizes the foundation work and prepares your house for the next, dramatic step of Dynamizing and staging. A house with neutral paint colors, decor, and carpeting will accommodate anyone's decorating style.

> **Creating a clean, new feeling can make your bottom line shine.**

Any strong decorating element, whether or not it is attractive, stops buyers so that they notice and remember the statement rather than the house. For example, an artist friend of mine displayed her work in her house. Her artwork is spectacular—revealing, full of emotion, and thought provoking. I wasn't surprised, however, when she confided to me that she was having trouble selling her home. Much as I love her artwork, I recommended that she take it down because I knew it would require a special buyer to be able to look beyond her work and *see* her house.

The same goes for political or religious statements that are so personal they make people feel like they are intruding on your privacy or uncomfortable if they disagree with the statement. Again, you don't want buyers focusing on your decorating. You want them to see and love your house. If a home is very much tailored to a specific individual, buyers experience trouble imagining their own things in that environment. Even large groups of family photographs can be intimidating. A few nicely framed pictures feel comfortable and homelike, but a shrine of personal photos makes buyers feel like intruders.

> **Distracting colors, accessories, and odors prevent a buyer from visualizing their things in your house.**

Any pets that live in your house will cause a strong, possibly negative statement, too. Research shows that half of all potential buyers are either allergic to, dislike, or are afraid of pets. Pets not only drag dirt into your house, they carry a distinct odor. Chances are you don't notice the smell as it's part of your everyday life, but animal scents will definitely reach your buyers. If they are allergic, they can't go on; if they are afraid, they won't go on.

Your house should offer as neutral or transparent an environment as possible so a buyer can find his dream house in yours. Unnerving artwork, loud paint colors, or a lurking animal can cause the buyer to fasten on these as negatives, ignoring the really positive aspects of your home. While you may have scoured the globe and paid a fortune for the highly patterned plaid wallpaper in your entrance hall, potential buyers may find it distracting. If they don't like it the first time they see it, you can be

> **Half of all buyers are allergic to, dislike, or are afraid of pets.**

sure that they won't want to imagine coming home to it every day. Again, most people are not particularly good at visualizing different furnishings or arrangements of furniture in a house, so they tend to think that what they see is what they get.

Remember, the elimination of personal tastes, strong colors, and posters, pictures, or other accessories that may distract or even be offensive makes it easier for buyers to imagine themselves living there. You may love a certain color or pattern, but if it doesn't fit a buyer's furniture or lifestyle, it's another reason for them to look elsewhere. Neutralizing your house increases the number of potential buyers for your house by appealing to as many different lifestyles as possible.

> **Buyers tend to think that what they see is what they get.**

NEUTRALIZE WALLS AND FLOORS

Neutralize dated or bold wallpaper and carpets. Removing wallpaper with a rented steamer is easy, quick, and inexpensive; then, paint the walls a light neutral color. Carpeting, a more expensive replacement, might be well worth the investment if the existing carpeting is extremely worn, unresolvably stained, or out of style. If there are wood floors—especially appealing to today's buyers—underneath old carpet, throw out the coverings and refinish the floors. If not, install a neutral sisal or Berber-type carpet. Make sure the floor and wall coverings enhance one another. For example, freshly painted walls will be lost against a bright green shag carpet. New carpeting and freshly painted walls will set your house firmly at the top of the price range—possibly even pushing you into a higher bracket.

NEUTRALIZE WITH PAINT

Painting is the most dramatic Neutralizing action. A fresh coat of light, neutral-color paint not only makes a room feel larger, it further enhances the feeling of clean, fresh, and new. Paint rooms that flow together—living room, dining room, kitchen, and hallways—the same color to heighten the feeling of expansiveness. When in doubt, use white paint. At the least, white is a perfect undercoat for a buyer's own taste. If she does want to paint, she'll surely recognize that it will be easy to do since you applied a base coat. Although she may not *choose* white, she won't *object* to it.

Paint gives the biggest bang for your buck.

A woman who attended one of my seminars complained that she was having trouble selling her house and couldn't understand why offers weren't rolling in. She had spent a great deal of time and money decorating and absolutely loved the results. Enthusiastically she described her favorite feature in the house—the kitchen. It had been completely updated, but she talked mainly about the fabulous paint color she had chosen to show off the room—a striking orange! As we talked further, she told of the other bold paint combinations throughout the house. I suggested that she try painting the walls an off-white. Result: The house sold within a week of painting.

Paint can work miracles on dull and dated cabinetry as well.

In a house I staged several years ago, a tiny, dark kitchen was transformed into a bright, cheery room simply by painting the cabinets a gleaming white and adding brass knobs.

Although real estate professionals will always recommend the safety of white, and I follow that rule for the main rooms of the house, I prefer slightly more dramatic, luxurious neutral colors, such as gray green or gray blue, for bedrooms, bathrooms, and dens. Once I staged a room by replacing bright lemon-yellow walls with a soft taupe color against white woodwork. The simple but striking change to a warmer, more inviting color made it easier to feel right at home. Neutralizing doesn't have to and shouldn't look boring.

Neutral doesn't have to be boring.

Remember the tiny bathroom with the dated gray jungle wallpaper and pink and gray tiles? I tried to neutralize it by removing the distracting wallpaper and painting the walls a pale gray green, resulting in a neutral but dull room. I was in the paint store and noticed a wallpaper display. One print caught my eye—the background was an off-white, with different shades of gray-green ivy and flowers with just a hint of burgundy. I took home a sample and marveled at the difference it made in that bathroom. The wallpaper made the bathroom a "dynamic" neutral. The shades of gray played off the gray tile, and the touch of burgundy made the pink tile look planned. I could easily have left the neutral paint color on the bathroom walls and saved the $50 I spent on wallpaper, but I'm certain that the dynamic impact of that wallpaper was worth the investment. It made a lasting positive impression of "What a charming bathroom!"

NEUTRALIZING ON A PERSONAL NOTE

The most common way of personalizing a home is the display of family photographs on tables, walls, and even refrigerators. It reinforces an atmosphere of togetherness and serves as a joyful reminder of cherished times and dear friends. Family photos are, however, too personal to display when selling your house because they distract buyers from the business at hand. Remove and pack personal photographs away while your house is on the market. A photo in an interesting frame on a bedside table or on an end table suggests a homey atmosphere. More than that is too personal.

NEUTRALIZE ODORS

Neutralizing goes deeper than just paint colors and accessories. It includes Neutralizing the way your house smells. While living in a house, people become accustomed to how it smells. You may not detect odors, so ask a trusted friend or neighbor to give your house the sniff test. Certain odors almost everyone finds offensive include those of mildewed basements, tobacco, pets, and cooking with garlic, curries, and fish. Run a dehumidifier in the basement to extract the dampness that causes mildew. Smoke outside on porches or decks. Refrain from cooking strong-smelling foods until after the sale. Keep an open box of baking soda in the refrigerator and freezer. Continue using lemon-scented cleaning products and keep windows open to ensure a fresh, clean aroma all through the house.

A buyer's nose knows.

GET RID OF PESTS

Another critical and often overlooked topic is pests. If you have insects like ants or pests like rodents in or around your house, get rid of them, professionally if necessary. A client had a house in a heavily wooded area and lamented that springtime always brought out the woodland pests—mice, ants, beetles, bees, and more. Although the family hadn't seen any of these pests

Buyer's don't want
a home that is
already occupied.

HOW MUCH DOES IT COST TO NEUTRALIZE?

The costs of Neutralizing should not be exhorbitant unless the house is extremely dated or worn. One way to economize is to paint rooms yourself. Otherwise, budget $500 to $1,000 to hire a painter depending on the size of your space.

The list below shows what it cost to Neutralize the last house I sold, and will give you an idea of the kinds of Neutralizing expenses you can expect.

Strip bathroom wallpaper, repaper	$50.00	Paint living room, dining room, kitchen, and hallway	215.00
"Mistake" paint in bathroom	25.00	New carpet in rec. room (15′ × 21′)	420.00
Basement wall and ceiling paint	100.00	Exterminator	125.00
Paint interior of all closets	40.00		
Touch up woodwork throughout	20.00	**Total Neutralizing costs**	**$995.00**

in the house during the last year or so, they were nervous. I recommended they have an exterminator do a thorough check of the house, and sure enough, he found signs of mice. Without that inspection, a family of scampering mice may have arrived uninvited at the Open House. Don't let pests drive away good prospects, especially when a quick call to the exterminator can alleviate the problem.

With your list of Neutralizing activities, prepare a budget of materials and labor. If you plan to hire help and the costs are larger than your pocketbook, prioritize with the four critical first-impression areas foremost: curb appeal, the entryway, the kitchen, and the bathrooms. If you're not sure which expenditures will provide the greatest return on investment, consult your real estate professional, who knows what's important to buyers in your area.

A FINAL NOTE

Avoid potential conflict by removing personal fixtures—the antique chandelier, the wall sconces your grandmother gave you—before putting your house on the market. If a potential buyer falls in love with a treasure that's moving with you, an argument and/or a painful negotiation may ensue. Neutralize by replacing these fixtures with stand-ins before the house is shown.

Pack your favorites now so you don't have to bargain for them later.

NEUTRALIZING, INSIDE AND OUT

Exterior/Curb Appeal

❑ If your house needs painting, now is definitely the time. It's an investment you should recoup. If you don't want to paint the whole house, consider giving it a facelift by painting just the trim.

❑ Neatly trim around a fire hydrant or municipal post-office box or lamppost. If it's an eyesore, contact your city to request permission to paint.

❑ Remove any visually distracting lawn accessories or ornaments.

❑ _____

❑ _____

Entryway

❑ Remove dated wallpaper. Paint with a neutral color.

❑ Replace lightbulbs.

❑ _____

❑ _____

Kitchen

- ❑ Eliminate odors from cooking oil, gas, and strong spices.

- ❑ Remove dated or bold wallcovering.

- ❑ If your wood cupboards are dated or worn, a coat of white enamel paint can transform them "instantly" and make the room feel larger and brighter.

- ❑ Flooring: If it's worn or dated, replace with neutral linoleum.

- ❑ _____

- ❑ _____

Bathrooms

- ❑ Paint or wallpaper in a neutral color.

- ❑ Use neutral shower curtain and towels.

- ❑ _____

- ❑ _____

Bedrooms

- ❑ Paint a restful neutral color.

- ❑ Remove distracting posters and other personalized belongings.

- ☐ _____

- ☐ _____

Living Room/Dining Room/Family Room

- ☐ Walls and ceilings: Paint a neutral color. Paint rooms that flow together the same color.

- ☐ Remove distracting posters or art. If you have a "collection" wall, pare it down and rearrange it. Make certain that frames line up at the top, bottom, and sides for a gallery look.

- ☐ _____

- ☐ _____

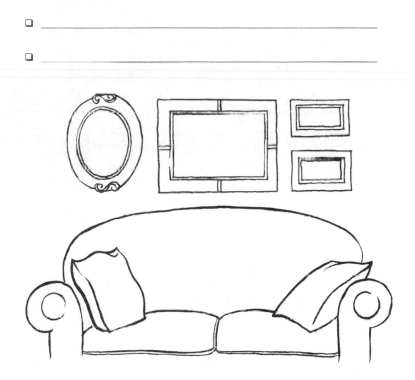

Basement/Garage/Attic

❑ Consider painting the walls white and the floors gray. It will help buyers see possibilities for additional uses.

❑ Paint the laundry room if it's in the basement.

❑ Add clip-on lights in an attic to enhance visibility.

❑ Replace dated carpeting with a neutral Berber style.

❑ If you have dated paneling, consider painting it for a more up-to-date "washed" cottage look.

❑ _____

❑ _____

8

STEP FIVE: DYNAMIZING

CONGRATULATIONS. There's just one more step to go before ShowTime! With hard work, you've created a sense of spaciousness, cleanliness, good repair, and low maintenance. Now, produce that even stronger feeling of *home* and *lifestyle* in your house. Dynamizing is my real secret weapon as well as my trademark. The goal of Dynamizing is to create a memorable feeling that lasts beyond the tour and makes a buyer want to come back to your house . . . to live. With methodical and imaginative Dynamizing you create impressionable moments when a buyer looks through a door in your house, enters a room, or even a closet, and something extraordinary occurs.

Bear in mind that buyers are looking for a house that meets their physical and psychological needs. If the first four steps—Uncluttering, Cleaning, Repairing, and Neutralizing—speak to their physical needs, step five, Dynamizing, reaches the psychological needs of home buyers. They want to feel comfortable, to enjoy a place of beauty and harmony, a haven from the hustle of daily living, a space to be proud

Small touches touch deep feelings.

to show family and friends. To succeed at selling your house quickly and profitably, you'll need to evoke those very feelings. Successful Dynamizing, like any kind of emotional communication, is strongest when you appeal to all the senses: not only vision, but touch, smell, hearing, even taste. By Dynamizing, or staging, little areas throughout the house, you ensure that buyers are constantly surprised and pleased at what they find, such as a glass vase filled with elegant roses greeting them in the entryway or the good smells of baking in the kitchen or a playfully arranged stuffed-animal tea party in a child's room.

REMEMBER POSITIONING

As you move through your house with buyer's eyes and the checklist from each chapter, keep in mind that your job as a marketer requires positioning your house to appeal to the broadest market possible. Ask "What about my house will appeal to buyers and why? Is it well suited for entertaining? Is it ideal for a growing family or better suited for a quieter, more intimate lifestyle?"

When making staging decisions, keep in mind that every buyer has different needs. Dynamizing a room to project only one function, therefore, limits its appeal. For example, in my last house, our office/den had actually been a fourth bedroom. The previous owners converted it to a TV room by adding oak paneling, a wall of built-in bookcases, and a built-in TV/entertainment center. I had used the room as an office, furnishing it with a desk, an easychair and ottoman, a floor lamp, and a file cabinet. When we decided to sell, I wanted to advertise the house as a four-bedroom and needed to demonstrate this den could work as an extra bedroom. I packed away half of the books from the bookshelves, freeing the space for display purposes. I uncluttered, cleaned, and painted the closet, replacing the file cabinet with a shelf on one side to expose a clothing rod so a buyer could imagine

> **Help a buyer see beyond what is to what can be.**

the space as either office storage or a clothing closet. Removing the heavy Roman shade, which made the room feel like a den, and adding miniblinds made the room feel lighter and more open. As it turned out, the family who bought the house needed that former office and den for a child's bedroom. Would they have been able to imagine it as a fourth bedroom if I hadn't dynamized? Probably not.

Dynamizing gives you the upper hand, the competitive edge, in any real estate market. Every space inside and outside of your house is a communication opportunity. While the first four steps have sent buyers one message, Dynamizing adds an even stronger message, suggesting easy living, convivial gatherings, or an abundance of personal time. Staging a kitchen area with an open cookbook, simmering spices, and a beautiful display of vegetables, invites buyers to imagine the good times and warm feelings that lay in store. When your house is the one buyers lose their hearts to, the competition doesn't stand a chance. Dynamizing isn't hard or expensive if you tackle it in three parts. Here's how to do it.

HOW MUCH WILL IT COST TO DYNAMIZE MY HOUSE?

What you spend on Dynamizing is entirely up to you. To minimize costs, borrow props whenever possible. If you end up purchasing "show" items such as colorful dish towels, lush comforters, flowering houseplants, and more, keep in mind that these items will go with you to your new home. Items that won't travel, or that you can't borrow and don't have the money or desire to purchase, can be rented at a fraction of their purchase price.

In general, though, don't be afraid to invest in this step; it pays for itself many times over. In a recent house that sold for $17,500 more than experts thought was possible, I spent a total of $755 on Dynamizing, most of which went with me to my new house. Here's a list of props and what they cost.

New entry rug	$35.00	Fresh mulch for flower beds	25.00
Roses for Open House	25.00	Flowers	150.00
Guest-room comforter, pillows	150.00	Window box plantings	50.00
Recreation room accessories	25.00	New towels, master and upstairs baths	100.00
Back-hall table (borrowed)	-0-	Flowering plant	15.00
Artwork for bare walls (borrowed)	-0-	Silk plant	25.00
Miniblinds to replace Roman shades	50.00	Place mats, napkins rings	35.00
Track lighting to replace dated fixture in entryway	45.00	Dish towels	25.00
		Total Dynamizing costs	**$755.00**

PART 1: IDENTIFY YOUR FIRST IMPRESSIONS

To start, shoot a roll of film, identifying different areas within and outside of your house. These thirty-six vignettes become key positioning points. Work methodically through the entire house.

Begin by taking a photograph of the first glimpse a buyer will have of your house. If that initial view is blocked by a movable obstruction such as a car in a neighbor's driveway, make arrangements to have the vehicle moved during showings to ensure an unobstructed view of your house. If that first glimpse includes an unattractive item that can't be moved, such as a fire hydrant or mailbox, plant bushes nearby (check your city regulations first) to mask it from view or arrange to have it painted to look better. Contact the city; it's their responsibility to keep fire hydrants well maintained.

> Use photos to create a blueprint for Dynamizing.

Next, stand across the street in front of your house—or building if you're selling an apartment or condominium—and take a picture of your curb appeal. Think about those critical first fifteen seconds when a buyer forms an opinion about your house. Everything that appears in the picture will contribute to a buyer's first impression and set the stage for the entire tour.

Now, walk through the house taking the route a buyer will follow and snap a photograph of the first glimpse of each room and area. The best way to do this is to back away from the doorframe until the doorway itself fills as much of the viewfinder of the camera as is possible. What you see is the image you'll be working with to create a first impression in every room.

Also take a photograph of the focal point—the architectural feature that most strongly attracts or pulls your eye—in each room. This could be a fireplace, bay window, stairway, or bookcase. Snap a photograph of any other areas that you find especially appealing and may want to highlight.

As you leave each room, take a picture, too, to see where the buyers' eyes lead. What do they see when they turn a corner? As they walk up or down stairs? All of these are first-impression opportunities.

Rush your film to a one-hour photo developer and get ready to outsmart your competition!

PART 2: EVALUATE YOUR OPPORTUNITIES

With your photographs spread out in order from first glimpse through the entire tour, evaluate the message your house sends. Carefully view each impression with buyer's eyes, anticipating how buyers will respond. Make it a game. Look at each picture and ask yourself or a friend, "What's wrong with this picture?" Then suggest ways to correct the impression. Does it make a statement now that supports the sense of home to the broadest number of buyers? If you answer yes, look one last time for opportunities to add special touches that will strengthen your positioning. If you notice from the photographs that an impression point doesn't support the overall positioning of

Design your set to appeal to all the senses.

that room, change your set. For example, the landing in a split-level house I recently dressed was immaculate—clean, spacious, and freshly painted a warm off-white. It looked great! Or so I thought until I laid out the photographs. When seen in a photograph, that landing looked and felt stark. As a place of entry and welcome to the main living level, it needed to exude warmth and comfort. And it didn't take much effort to Dynamize this impression point. I added a beautiful wood

table with a lamp, and a picture above the table. With the lamp turned on, the polished wood added a warm glow and spotlighted the eye-level picture, focusing a buyer's eyes on a particularly "homey" scene. The final touch—a nosegay of roses in a glass vase—was placed on the table to add elegance and a sense of owner pride in the house.

Keep in mind that the more senses—sight, sound, smell, touch—you reach with your message, the more successful your communication. As you move through the house Dynamizing, utilizing props and staging techniques, keep asking yourself "What will the buyer see? How will she respond?"

PART 3: STAGE FOR THE MESSAGE

Look at the pictures you clipped from decorating magazines or home-furnishing catalogs. The rooms send warm messages of family togetherness without any visible people. Photographed homes look and feel like the perfect place to bake cookies, relax, and take life at a slower pace, lulling in the tranquillity of old-fashioned family values. Your challenge involves invoking the same feelings.

Start in each room thinking about what feeling matches what room, considering ease, abundance, newness, comfort, relaxation, organization, fun, spaciousness, luxury, and excitement. For example, a kitchen should feel functional and organized and suggest that meal preparation is easy and enjoyable. A bedroom should send a message of relaxation and refuge.

> **A picture is worth a thousand words. An impression is invaluable.**

CHECK OUT SIGHT LINES

As you begin to set your stage, attend to the larger, main pieces of furniture in each room first to guide the buyer's views, then play with the smaller touches.

Remember that all the furniture in each room need not stay in that room; you can move pieces around or store them. Use furniture to guide buyers gracefully through your house. If they have to walk around a piece of furniture to enter a room, then it creates a negative feeling of clutter and obstructs a critical first-impression point. When the furniture placement is right, buyers easily and comfortably walk into each room. Don't allow furniture to erect physical barriers preventing a buyer from seeing the flow of your house.

Use furniture to usher a buyer into a room.

In the town house that sold before the other two also for sale in the complex, I staged a third bedroom that was being used as an office/study. As you can see from this rough floor plan, each wall of that little office was cluttered with filing cabinets, a large desk, typing table, and other items. A tall bookcase directly obstructed the sight line from the doorway. Consequently, the room felt small and cramped. As a workspace, it felt crowded and frustrating, and there was no sign of a potential bedroom.

Opening the closet doors and moving the file cabinets inside gained space and widened the buyer's line of vision. Angling the desk directly under the window made the room feel immediately bigger because it freed up more wall

Opening doors can open possibilities.

BASIC FURNITURE PLACEMENT GUIDELINES

Create a sense of spaciousness, warmth, and comfort with the following suggestions:

✔ Match size of furniture with size of space. A large table in a small corner will make a room feel crowded. Likewise a small chest of drawers against a large wall will feel awkward and lost.

✔ Place heavy, oversize furniture across the room from other large, heavy furniture for a well-balanced feel. Keep heavy furniture away from doorways and entry sight lines.

✔ Bring furniture into the room rather than lining it up against the wall like wallflowers.

✔ Angle furniture in a small room to make it feel larger. Place furnishings at an angle in an empty room to add variety and interest.

✔ Avoid competing focal points such as a large entertainment center on a fireplace wall, which create an imbalance in the room.

✔ Use area rugs to define specific areas. They are not meant to "float" in the middle of a room.

✔ Create sight lines in a room by arranging furniture to flow from low to high. For example, arrange furniture so that the eye moves from a low end table to a chair and on to a bookcase. This one smooth eye movement creates an orderly feeling.

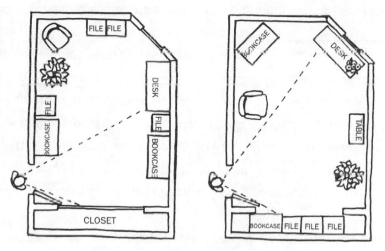

ABOVE: Rearranging the furniture widens a room's sight lines.

space. Fresh flowers on the desktop drew the eye to the window and beyond, giving the illusion of expansive space. Keeping the closet open suggested the possible use of the room as a bedroom. Overall, with the same space and the same furniture, I created an impression of more usable space and greater flexibility, implying greater ease of living.

That's the power of Dynamizing!

USING PROPS TO ENHANCE THE MESSAGE

Once the larger pieces are in place, work with art and accessories to complete the overall impression and convey subtle messages. By directing a buyer's eyes with well-placed accessories, you actually mount a layered process of discovery. Dynamizing can light up your house, moving buyers along a well-lit path, exposing the types of lifestyle your house supports.

Keep it simple. Buyers will be drawn into a room with a

touch as light as a bouquet of flowers strategically placed in a sight line near the door. A bouquet can

Accessorize to engage buyers in discovering the potential of your house.

also direct a buyer's eyes to the next area or room. The effects are cumulative: Placing a book by a table on the sunporch suggests relaxing time to read; a game set out in the family room underscores that yours is a family house; a freshly painted, well-organized broom closet proclaims that even daily chores are easily accomplished here.

A few strategically placed props powerfully enhance a space and evoke positive feelings. However, overloading accessories results in clutter that can overwhelm and distract the buyer. Prevent cluttering when you distribute props by obeying the rule of threes. When placing items on a tabletop, in a corner, or against a wall, do so in groups of three. Make sure the three

items are different in height and volume for visual interest. Watch the proportions, using smaller items on smaller tables and taller items on larger tables. Three carefully chosen items

Propping is as easy as one, two, three

will add drama and heighten placement effects. Fewer than three can feel incomplete; more will be too busy.

Plants and Flowers

Use plants and flowers to bring the outdoors in and infuse any room with beauty and grace. The simple elegance of a dozen roses, for example, shows the pride owners take in their house and feels especially welcoming to buyers. In a condominium or apartment complex, donate a large blooming plant for the building's entry. A bare corner can sport combined green and flowering plants in groups of three, or a basket of plants near a window or on top of a small table make any room come alive.

Closets

Purchase wood hangers for a front-hall closet and make sure all contents hang in the same direction. Group same-size jackets together for a spacious, organized look. In bedroom closets use clear storage boxes stacked neatly on shelves. Carefully line up shoes on a rack underneath clothing. They'll look orderly and ready to be used at a moment's notice—no searching around for shoes in this house.

Make linen closets look as neat and well-organized as a linen shop by tri-folding and carefully stacking sheets, blankets, and towels so no seams or edges show. Stack twin, full, queen-, and king-size sheets and blankets together. Include attractive sachets for an especially pleasing look and scent. A well-staged closet or storage room has a major impact on buyers. Install organizers to bring items up off the floor, and use racks, hooks, and holders to ensure a specific place for every item.

DYNAMIZING, INSIDE AND OUT

As you work through your house, you'll find numerous Dynamizing opportunities to deliver subtle messages of home and build an atmosphere of excitement for buyers. Here are Dynamizing ideas that can work in any house.

Exterior/Curb Appeal

Remember, a buyer forms an attitude about your house within fifteen seconds. For that reason, curb appeal is the most important first impression, and encompasses everything from the street corner all the way up to the chimney.

If you're selling an apartment or condominium, look at the image presented by your building and adapt these curb appeal steps to create excitement in your potential buyers, to bring them to your unit in eager anticipation.

Greet buyers with dynamic curb appeal:

❑ Add splashes of color and beauty to welcome buyers. You don't have to be a master gardener to accomplish a few plantings.

- Place potted plants at the front door and annuals along the walk or in clusters around a lamppost or tree. Overplant to create an instant lush, flourishing look. In colder climates, an evergreen in a pot will make for a warm greeting.

- Place a hanging flowering plant at eye level to add grace to a front entry, porch, or patio.

- Group for drama. I lined a brick patio with clay pots planted identically with begonias and impatiens. It's much more dramatic than a single pot.

- Look around your yard. Are there bare spots that could benefit from a few inexpensive plants? I had an area under a small pine tree that came alive with the addition of six begonias. Impatiens are perfect under and between shrubs.

- If you have window boxes, plant fully with greens and flowers to create a flourishing, luxuriant look. If you don't have them, they are easy to install on brackets or a porch railing and give a dressed-up look to any house. Place them outside windows in condos and apartments. If it is winter, add treetops and pinecones to dress up an empty window box.

❑ Add fresh wood chips or gravel around trees and shrubs for a well-manicured appearance.

❑ Make your mailbox picture-perfect. If it's an eyesore, replace it or paint it and the pole and add new, bold numbers for visibility and clarity. It's a subtle indication of good maintenance.

❑ A front door is more than just an entry to your home; it's the focal point of your house and a place of welcome. Your efforts here will set the stage for the inside tour. Choose ideas that will enhance the entrance to your house:

- Consider a fresh coat of paint or a carefully applied wood polish on your front door to make it feel bright and welcoming.

- Polish the hardware so it gives a shining, lustrous impression.

- Add a gleaming new door knocker.

- Add an all-season wreath.

- Add drama by flanking the door with planters and/or large plants, such as topiary trees.

- A new, up-to-date light fixture by the front door can be an inexpensive way to add real style to the entranceway.

❑ Add shutters to dress up a facade.

❑ Add shiny new brass house numbers or a cast-iron address plate.

❑ A clean, new doormat is guaranteed to be noticed.

❑ If your car will be in the driveway, have it washed and waxed.

❑ Evaluate outdoor lighting. During dark months, your house may be shown at dusk. The warm glow of walkway lights will add drama to your entrance.

❑ _____

❑ _____

Entryway

This small area is to the interior of a house as curb appeal is to the exterior. It plays a significant role in setting the tone for the entire tour.

- ❏ Enhance and add drama by showcasing a unique piece of furniture or artwork; group a small table and a colorful vase to suggest elegance.

- ❏ Greet your buyers with grace and beauty. A fresh floral bouquet is dramatic and makes a buyer feel especially welcome. It also conveys a sense of the owner's pride in the house. In an apartment or condominium build-

ing, donate a blooming plant or an artificial arrangement for the entry.

❑ Place a new, dramatic throw rug in the entry to add warmth, texture, and color, making sure to secure it with a pad underneath to hold it firmly in place. It softens the entry and has a much more welcoming feel than bare floor. Over carpet, it adds dimension and the "layering" effect creates a feeling of comfort.

❑ Install a gleaming, new brass switchplate.

❑ If a lighting fixture is dated or worn, a new halogen one will cast a dramatic, focused light to highlight an important area while also adding style to a tired-looking or unexciting entry.

❑ _____

❑ _____

Kitchen

Definitely the most important room in the house, the kitchen also happens to be the easiest to Dynamize. It can take center stage when you focus on quick and inexpensive changes rather than extensive improvements.

❑ On a clean, clear counter, set a cookbook open on a stand. Place a cheerful flowering plant next to it to suggest enjoyment of meal preparation and the warm spirit of entertaining.

- Purchase bright new dish towels and pot holders. Roll them in a flowerpot or wicker basket next to the sink. Accent with a raffia bow for added texture and a finished look.

- Add color with new burner covers, and at the same time create a neat, clean look.

- Add a new soap holder.

- Create a high-tech look with track lighting.

- Add a new area rug. Store it in a closet between showings to keep it looking clean and fresh.

❏ Place fresh fruit in a stand. Be sure to replace any that gets old or soft.

❏ Keep a blooming plant on the table or in the window.

❏ Window treatments: Replace worn curtains with mini-blinds or a bold valance to add drama.

❏ Dynamize a kitchen table:

  • Use a tiered holder or pretty bowl as a centerpiece to display colorful fresh fruit. Include grapes because they drape well, giving a more relaxed feel to the arrangement.

  • Purchase a set of informal show place mats and napkins that match the kitchen decor and state casual elegance and mealtime fun. These will highlight the eating area without overpowering the room.

❏ During an Open House, set out a serving tray with matching cups and napkins and a pitcher of lemonade. Add a plate of cookies and invite families to share a snack. This encourages prospective buyers to linger in the kitchen, talk, enjoy themselves, and to feel as if they belong in your house.

❏ A makeover does not have to be expensive. Freshening what you already own can have a substantial impact on your selling price and market time.

- Add molding to plain cabinets to create a richer feeling. Or consider the services of a kitchen "tune-up" company to generate a current and up-to-date look.

- Install new hardware for a dressed-up look. The variety in kitchen knobs and pulls is astounding. This is an easy way to update and add interest to a kitchen at minimal expense.

- If your counters are dark, replace them with a light, neutral top for a more universal appeal and cheerful feeling.

❑ _____

❑ _____

Bathrooms

Bathrooms run the risk of being small and dull because they're so functional, yet buyers yearn for a bigger shower, a larger tub. So, if yours looks spacious, clean, and in good repair, your buyers will have another "found" on their list of "must haves." Convey luxury and relaxation:

❑ Fill a shell with small, subtly scented soaps, and place a bottle of herb-scented bath oil on the tub ledge with a thick, sumptuous towel draped over the side.

❑ Purchase show towels in a combination of neutral and bold colors to soften the room and add texture. Fold in thirds to hide edges and seams. Hang in layers on a towel rack and roll remaining towels for display purposes in a floor basket or on a vanity. The layering creates a luxurious feeling in a room that is often stark and cold.

- Open a bathroom window if your bathroom has one, and place a small bouquet of fresh flowers or an aloe plant on the sill or vanity. Choose an innovative vase such as a little pitcher, antique bottle, or interesting candy tin. The fresh, cheerful image of flowers combined with the pleasant surprise of the curious little vase will position the bathroom in the buyer's mind as a fresh, beautiful space.

- A new shower curtain adds inexpensive drama, texture, and luxury to a bathroom. Purchase, borrow, or create a two-paneled curtain and valance for a luxurious impact. If the bathroom is small, use curtain tiebacks to open up the space and draw the eye as far back as possible.

- Replace a dated or worn light fixture. Add a vanity strip for a current look.

- Reenamel an old, chipped tub to bring your bathroom quickly into vogue.

- Add new towel racks to match fixtures (silver, brass, or wood).

- Add bathroom potpourri, a scented candle, and guest soaps.

- Select a few items with more decorative packaging (perfumes, lotions, soaps) to place in a basket on a ledge. Make sure everything in it is sparkling clean.

- _____

- _____

Bedrooms

Showcase tranquillity and a restful haven with simple touches. Remember purchases here will move with you to set a new stage in your new home.

- Dynamize a nightstand by placing a crisp linen or cotton table runner over the top. Arrange a hardcover book near a small vase with flowers, a photograph, and an attractive reading lamp.

- Borrow or purchase a plush new comforter. Add panache with decorative pillows and shams.

- Hang a mirror to create a feeling of spaciousness. By placing it directly across from a window you collect and reflect the most light and bring in the peaceful, expansive feeling of the outdoors.

- Add a group of green and flowering plants in an empty space.

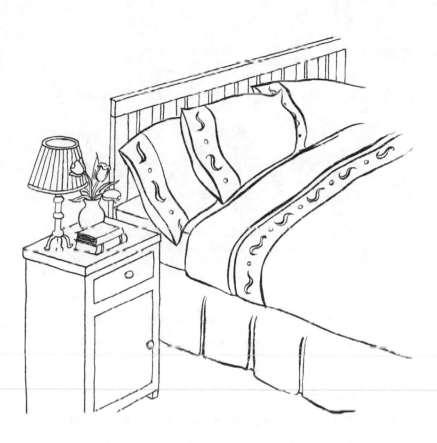

❏ Add curtains and valances or miniblinds to windows without them.

❏ Add humor and fun to children's bedrooms by play-fully arranging toys and stuffed animals. Whether frolicking on the bed or marching in a line, stuffed animals are a great way to add whimsical humor to a child's bedroom.

- Consult and involve your children in arranging a fantasy dress-up corner, an artist's nook, a train track, and more.

- Set a toy or puzzle on the table in a child's room, but keep others out of sight. If you do not have a toy chest or toy storage area, use a laundry basket to keep the room neat.

- Purchase an inexpensive net-type hammock to hang across a corner to hold a stuffed-animal zoo.

❑ Evaluate the lighting. Consider replacing old or dated overhead fixtures or adding a ceiling fan.

❑ _____

❑ _____

Living Room/Family Room

Stage the warm, congenial feelings of family fun and togetherness, a room in which to entertain or enjoy the calm at the end of a day.

❏ Showcase a fireplace by placing logs in and around it. Use pretty white-bark birch logs for a more dramatic "at the lake" look. Stack kindling in a basket on the hearth to suggest the ease with which a warm, crackling fire can be produced. Add art above a fireplace or on the mantel to give a sense of height and prominence.

- Set a board game or jigsaw puzzle neatly on a table and add a big bowl of popcorn or colorful M&M's. Buyers will immediately see themselves playing that game, laughing, and munching the evening away.

- Stage a quiet space. Drape an afghan over an easychair, open a book on the ottoman or end table. Turn on a lamp next to the chair, or toss an afghan on a couch or armchair, suggesting leisure time to nap or cuddle. Plump all pillows, adding more if necessary

- Display a few visually interesting magazines in a magazine rack or on a coffee table, without creating clutter.

- Stage a bookcase. Place books vertically, horizontally, and face a few with interesting jackets. Add art objects and accessories to the shelves to create interest and demonstrate flexibility of use.

- Arrange artwork and furniture to highlight special features. For example, a group of vertical pictures on a small wall can enhance a bay window or a built-in buffet.

❏ Add a fresh bouquet of flowers or a European plant basket to a coffee table or sofa table. Display a vase or special dish to add elegance. Be cautious not to overdo it. You want buyers to feel the elegance, not browse as if they were shopping.

❏ If you have an entertainment center, keep doors closed and shelves neat and uncluttered. Keep televisions off.

❏ _____

❏ _____

Dining Room

Stage this room just enough to suggest how proud buyers would be to entertain here. Fuel their imagination without cluttering the room's elegance. Don't actually set a formal table, which looks manipulative. Buyers know you aren't going to have a dinner party as soon as they leave.

❏ Add accessories to a dining buffet, and group in threes for interest and drama. A lone vase looks bare, whereas a grouping of three items such as candles, an antique vase, and a small stack of books looks natural, almost haphazard. It engages the eye in an appealing, memorable way.

❏ Add a runner, a bouquet of flowers, and candles to a polished dining room table. Stack a set of coasters or display an interesting serving piece.

❑ Set tables in places that buyers might not think of for eating, such as an informal setting at a coffee table in an amusement room in front of a fireplace.

❑ _____

❑ _____

Basement/Laundry Area/Garage/Attic

These are areas most sellers ignore, but a few careful touches can ensure that buyers feel daily chores and maintenance will be hassle-free.

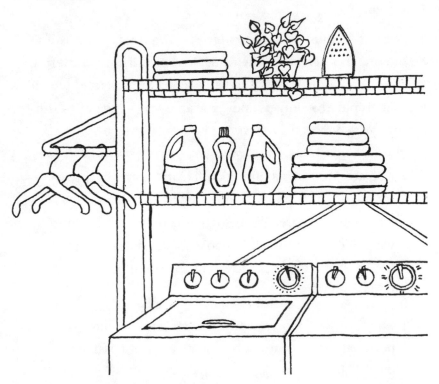

❑ Arrange laundry supplies in an orderly fashion to suggest that doing laundry here is quick and easy.

- Face all products.

- Add a wire shelving unit over the appliances if you don't have shelves.

- Add a green plant or artificial bouquet to make this area as cheerful as possible.

❑ Stage a hobby project on a work bench to suggest time and space to pursue personal activities and hobbies. By staging an actual work-in-progress, you jog buyers' minds to think of all they want to work on and how your house is the place to make those dreams a reality.

❑ _____

❑ _____

Backyard/Deck/Balcony

Create a resort look in your backyard or terrace to invoke feelings of friends and family gathered together.

❑ Arrange lawn furniture to suggest an outdoor barbecue. Place a table next to the grill with barbecue tongs, fork, and knife carefully laid out and ready. Borrow a croquet set and other lawn games and place them in a corner of the deck or patio to suggest hours of backyard fun.

- Arrange colorful pots of annuals in groupings on a deck. Set pots on steps.

- Arrange children's pool toys and games on a deck or in a gazebo.

- Fill bird feeders and make sure birdhouses look appealing. Paint the metal pole or the house itself if necessary. Add a fun, new bird feeder in the backyard. The selections today are entertaining and can add another element of interest to the yard.

- Re-stain a picnic table and add a pot of flowers as a centerpiece.

- In winter, consider making a snowman, complete with carrot nose, scarf, and top hat.

- In dark months, add white lights to trees or bushes to give a sense of depth after dusk.

- Add railing pots of blooming annuals to balconies.

- _____

- _____

9

SHOWTIME!

IF DYNAMIZING IS the overture to homeselling success, then ShowTime is the curtain-raiser, when your house is shown to prospective buyers. It is for this moment that all your labors have been expended, and if you have done your job properly, it should be the proof that my five-step program really gets results; with proper preparation, a realistic price, and a little bit of luck, you could have an offer in hand by the end of the day!

In preparing your house for its big debut, you're focused on the deadline: the Open House date or that first day on the market. Every effort up to now—Uncluttering, Cleaning, Repairing, Neutralizing, and Dynamizing—is aimed toward that important date. Then, moments before curtain time, just like a theatrical stage manager, you run down your final, last-minute checklist. To be absolutely certain that all of these important details are attended to, your master checklist will identify every crucial detail and ensure a successful show.

A SHOWTIME PLAN: STAYING READY

Your ShowTime plan will insure that when the curtain is raised, your house will be a star at every showing. House showings can really interrupt daily life, trying your time and patience, and your family might not always feel in control.

A no-stress plan for a sold-out show.

While ShowTime often happens at the last minute, it doesn't have to result in panic and additional stress. Follow my ShowTime rule: "By *staying* ready, you don't have to *get* ready." If the basic picking up and cleaning are done every morning, the house is nearly ready for showing *at all times*. Your ShowTime plan will include specific roles, tasks, and areas for each member of your household to maintain so everything moves like clockwork.

If you follow the program in this book, chances are good that you'll have a buyer soon after that first Open House. However, not every house sells at first; several showings might be needed before the right buyer walks through the door. When you have a plan to stay on top of last-minute staging details, frequent showings are less disruptive.

A friend tells a story of what typically happens when a house is actively on the market. Her house was in perfect shape; all of the steps were done, and she had just completed her ShowTime run-through on the downstairs rooms when the doorbell rang: The buyers and broker were half an hour early! Just then, her six-year-old ran downstairs and burst into tears. "Oh, Mom," he cried, "I tried cleaning up my room, but my clothes won't fit back in my dresser."

Sure enough, when my friend raced upstairs, she found clothes spilling out of the dresser in her son's room. She had seconds to sort through the chaos and return order to the room while her older child filled in as a greeter downstairs. One of a hundred ShowTime close calls!

Even though Realtors try to be sensitive, they often can't offer much notice before a buyer wants to see your house. Yet the house needs to be in perfect shape. Since my friend's family knew the roles each member needed to fill, it was easy for one to substitute for another unexpectedly.

WHERE TO BEGIN

Getting your home in ShowTime-ready condition is one thing; keeping it that way is another. Whether your house will be shown daily or you are working toward one or more open houses, you will need a gameplan that ensures all the work and effort you've invested over the past ten days is not undone. The list on page 154 gives a good idea of how to maintain that pristine, model-home look you've worked so hard to create, so your house never needs more than a quick final run through to be in perfect ShowTime shape. The list includes both significant jobs that should be performed on a weekly basis plus the smaller tasks that you will want to do *daily*.

A leading role for everyone.

Let each household member select an area or room, in addition to his or her own, to keep ready. If they are given a choice, they'll *feel* more involved in the responsibility. Make sure every-

STAYING READY CHECKLIST

WEEKLY OR BIWEEKLY

❑ Dust and vacuum at least once a week.

❑ Clean fingerprints from walls, woodwork, and glass.

❑ Scrub bathrooms to a shine.

❑ Avoid an accumulation of dirty laundry.

❑ Keep the lawn neatly mowed. Trim shrubs and flowers.

❑ If you live in snow country, keep walks well shoveled.

❑ Wipe down lawn furniture to look fresh and clean.

❑ Maintain pool or hot tub.

❑ Replenish interior flowers and plants for a fresh feel.

DAILY

❑ Make all beds before leaving the house. Set out bedroom staging items.

❑ Wipe down the shower or tub each morning. Put away all personal-care items. Wipe out sink.

❑ Make sure anything that was used is put back in its place: toys, games, sports equipment, newspapers, magazines.

❑ Clean up immediately after meals and stow all cooking utensils. Keep meals simple.

❑ Walk through and neaten the entire house before you depart.

❑ Survey the lawn and make sure all toys and equipment are carefully put away before leaving.

one knows *how* to get his or her job done and understands that the house must be cleaner and neater than ever before—for every showing. Show younger household members exactly what picking up your room looks like during this time and offer instructions for their own staging: which pillows to set out and exactly where on the bed to place them, which stuffed animals to arrange, how to Dynamize the top of a dresser or bedside table. You may still have to do a quick check, but it will make your job easier and all will feel that they have contributed to this important venture when they understand exactly what their roles are and how to accomplish them.

CREATE A SHOWTIME GAME

The key to ShowTime is to impart the spirit of showmanship to your entire household: It builds team spirit and adds a real sense of fun to this vital effort. Devise games to help ensure the house remains looking its absolute best. Give out awards in such categories as most organized, most innovative, staging, best lighting, most neutral, freshest smelling, greatest attention to detail, and best special effects; this way, everyone participating can win. If your household includes children, encourage cooperation, and use the ShowTime Game on page 174. Add prizes appropriate to your budget and the ages and interests of your family members. I've given prizes as varied as an ice cream sundae, a toy, a movie rental, and even double allowance when my kids have really pitched in to help prepare the house—and *kept* it that way. If your household consists of just you or another adult, decide on a reward that's extraspecial:

dinner at a fine restaurant, tickets to a play you've longed to see, or maybe even a trip you've been putting off. Finally, decide on a grand prize for the entire household to enjoy when you reach your goal—a SOLD sign majestically perched out front.

KEEP THE FINISHING TOUCHES FRESH

Stay on top of important staging details such as flowers, lighting, aromas, sounds, and room temperature, so you can get your house in ShowTime condition at a moment's notice. By constantly updating the little touches in and around your house, showing becomes almost hassle-free. Of course, not all of your staging elements can remain intact without maintenance for an extended time—flowers wilt, lovely baking smells dissipate, M&M's disappear, and outside temperatures change. Still, you'll want to be aware of when it's time to replenish and re-create.

Aromas

- Keep your house smelling as fresh as it is clean (the scent of lemon cleaning products remains in your house long after the cleaning). Also, leave your windows open whenever possible to let in the fresh-smelling air.

- Increase frequency of pet cleanup. Change litter boxes more often and arrange to have pets groomed regularly.

- If you'd like to add the smell of fresh baking, research shows that cinnamon is considered the most pleasing baking smell. Purchase several containers of ready-to-bake cinnamon rolls. They smell heavenly and require only a few minutes for preparation and cleanup.

Flowers

- You'll want to have larger flower arrangements for an Open House. For individual showings, maintain a few casual arrangements throughout the house.

- Use bedding plants in household containers such as baskets and serving dishes to stretch your budget and add interest. Nestle as many as you can inside the dish and cover the tops with moss to hide the bedding containers. The plants can last for up to two weeks, and when they begin looking tired, simply plant them outside. It revives the plants and adds to your curb appeal, too!

- Plant an assortment of herbs in an attractive basket to set by the kitchen sink. It not only looks inviting, it outlasts cut flowers and the herbs smell great, too.

- Indoor rock gardens are fun to create, add wonderful visual interest, and are maintenance-free.

Select a clear, shallow bowl and some interesting rocks. Float enough water to cover some but not all of the rocks. Add a single flowering bloom to float in the rock garden.

- Use seasonal flowers from your yard and a mixture of greens to add volume to your flower bouquets. A large bunch of lilacs will cover several rooms. Prolong the bouquets by changing the water daily. Remove and replace any wilted or tired-looking flowers.

Light

- Highlight areas that receive a lot of natural light. Place a vase or sculpture where it catches the sun.

- Keep blinds and drapes wide open for maximum light and cheer.

- Place lamps to brighten dark areas or spotlight terrific ones. Think of them as stage lighting. Try to limit the use of overhead lighting—it can be harsh. Individual lamps highlight specific staging elements that lead a buyer's eyes exactly where you want them to look.

Pets

- Make a plan to take pets with you when leaving the house. If that's too difficult, consider kenneling them while your house is on the market. If you leave them in the house during showings, they may sense something out of the ordinary and act up just as your potential buyer arrives. Remember, *up to half of all buyers are allergic to, dislike, or are afraid of pets.*

I recently had a frightening pet experience while looking at a house to purchase. I opened what I thought was a closet door but turned out to be the door to the basement. Before I could even see what was inside, a huge dog jumped out at me. I recovered quickly because I like dogs. However, I'm *not* fond of cats, and had it been a cat, I would have been clinging to the chandelier.

Valuables

- Play it safe. Don't leave valuables, including personal papers, in the house for showings. Why take the risk? Store your valuables with a friend or in a safety-deposit box.

THE FINAL CHECK

For this step you'll need the same two totes or baskets you used in the Cleaning step: one with cleaning supplies and one to pick up out-of-place items. Designate a specific place for ShowTime staging items such as show pillows, bathroom guest soaps, and more. A closet in the appropriate room works best. As you walk through the entire house, Cleaning and Uncluttering as needed, tick off items on your ShowTime checklist. You can use the checklist on page 162 or write your own personal ShowTime plan. Keep it with your cleaning supplies and pickup basket. Make sure every family member knows where

Places, everyone!

it is and what to do in case you're not available. Use this list on the final walk through before each and every showing.

As you run through this checklist, keep your goal in mind: a house that looks clean and feels new is one that is easy to explore and invites buyers to imagine it as their home. Pay special attention to the four critical first-impression areas: curb appeal, entryway, kitchen, and bathrooms.

THE SHOWING

Timing is everything. If you apply my stay-ready rule and keep up with the daily and weekly checklist of chores, you will be able to prepare your house for a showing in under an hour. However, if you do get a last-minute request and

Upstage your competition.

your house needs work, keep your cool. Ask the Realtor for the time you need to do a quick cleanup. Be honest. Say you want to show your house's best face. Don't be talked into showing your house in less-than-perfect condition. All your efforts leading up to then will be diminished if you let buyers see your house at less than its best.

Be realistic, too. If a buyer is in town for only a day and a

Realtor wants to show your house, get it ready as quickly as possible. As a seller, you need to go that extra mile to accommodate buyers' schedules; this is basic customer service. If you don't, I guarantee your competition will.

Leave the house during showings. Buyers are much more comfortable inspecting a house if the owner isn't there. They look deeper and talk more openly about the house.

If you're on the fence about listing your house with a real estate professional, the fact that Realtors are experienced at showing houses and answering buyers' questions may clinch your decision. I recommend leaving your house at ShowTime in the hands of a professional Realtor, who is experienced at pointing out highlights that sell your house. Many agents prepare a feature sheet that calls attention to the benefits of your house. Don't feel awkward about reminding your agent of special features you want pointed out. After an Open House or showing, be sure to discuss any feedback your agent received both from buyers and other agents. Listen objectively. Remain open and flexible. Remember, this is business. Your goal is to sell your house quickly and extremely profitably. Objectivity can provide you with valuable positioning information.

If you're selling the house yourself, let buyers guide themselves through your house. They'll feel freer to look around and discuss the house if you aren't within ear-shot. You'll want to be there to welcome them and answer questions, but let them explore the house through their own eyes. Make up a feature sheet highlighting special features of your house for buyers to

SHOWTIME CHECKLIST

EXTERIOR

- ☐ Pick up lawn tools and toys.
- ☐ Pick up after pets.
- ☐ Remove obstructions from curb view.
- ☐ Clear driveways and walk areas.
- ☐ Use a leaf blower or hose down walk areas for a neat and tidy look.
- ☐ Clear away debris from pool or hot tub.
- ☐ _____
- ☐ _____

INTERIOR

- ☐ Empty wastebaskets.
- ☐ Pick up dirty clothes.
- ☐ Clear papers and notes from desks, counters, and tables.
- ☐ Check for hazards—extension cords, throw rugs, etc.
- ☐ Put away personal-care items in bathrooms.
- ☐ Straighten and stage children's play areas.
- ☐ Do a once-over cleaning: Vacuum, sweep, and dust.
- ☐ Wipe down counters, sinks, and bathtubs. Finish with glass cleaner.

- ☐ Deodorize pet areas.
- ☐ Arrange fresh flowers throughout.
- ☐ Make sure rugs are straight and clean.
- ☐ Open shades and drapes.
- ☐ Open windows to freshen rooms.
- ☐ Turn on lights.
- ☐ Add the smell of fresh baking.
- ☐ _____
- ☐ _____

LAST-MINUTE DYNAMIZING

- ☐ Arrange tables with flowers and linens.
- ☐ Set out a game, book, hobby project.
- ☐ Arrange show towels in bathrooms and kitchens.
- ☐ Play soft music and turn off television.
- ☐ Set a comfortable temperature.
- ☐ Final check every room.
- ☐ Leave, and take your pet with you, or to the kennel.
- ☐ _____
- ☐ _____

take with them. A sample feature sheet is included as a guide (see page 172). Also consider using special-feature cards to draw attention to key areas of the house. For example:

SPECIAL FEATURE

★ ★ ★ ★ ★

ROLLOUT VANITY DRAWER
HIS & HERS ORGANIZERS

Be subtle about it. Too many of these will look like clutter. A few will make buyers take notice. Also have a sign-in sheet near the entrance with enough space for buyers' phone numbers and comments. You may want to contact some of these prospects for additional

> **Usher buyers through your house with a personal Playbill®.**

feedback. Or, if you decide to hire a Realtor after your house has been on the market, the Realtor may want to contact some of these prospects for their impressions.

GIVE BUYERS A LOOK AT LIFE IN YOUR NEIGHBORHOOD

Broaden the appeal of your house at ShowTime by providing buyers with information about your neighborhood and community. This can be as simple as a clean copy of the listing, a color photo of the house, and a brief description of the neighborhood (see page 172 for an example). Or it can be a much grander production, including a special binder, a color cover with photographs of the house in various seasons, and several pages of neatly printed information about the neighborhood, community services, local schools, neighboring families, local parks and activities, your favorite video store and dry cleaner. These details can make buyers feel they will fit right in. The prospect of living in your house, on your street, and in your community will seem especially enticing. Include the following:

- ❏ **NEIGHBORHOOD INFORMATION.** List the number and ages of children on the street, along with a summary of adults' occupations and interests. If there is an active neighborhood association, include information on membership and activities.

- ❏ **SCHOOL AND DAY CARE INFORMATION.** Write a paragraph about the quality of the schools using information obtained from the school district. Most districts have preprinted information they can send you. List both public and private preschool, elementary, middle, and high schools. Include information on school-bus pickups.

- ❏ **BABY-SITTERS.** Include number (quantity) available.

- ❏ **RECREATIONAL INFORMATION.** Obtain maps and information on area parks and a catalog of local activities. Include a section of movie theaters, playhouses, museums, and libraries in the community.

❑ **LOCAL RETAILERS.** List your favorite merchants: dry cleaner, video store, grocery store, pharmacy, hairdresser, pet groomer, and more. Add a section on restaurants and include a variety from fast food and delis to popular family spots and fine dining.

❑ **UTILITIES.** Buyers appreciate knowing what costs they can expect beyond just the mortgage. Gather copies of bills or create a full-year list by month of heat and electric expenditures. This demonstrates a willingness to provide complete and accurate information that will help buyers make a decision that *feels* rational and informed.

❑ **A PERSONAL LETTER.** Write a letter to buyers expressing what you have especially liked about living here: the neighbors, special household features such as how perfect the backyard and deck have been for casual and impromptu entertaining. Briefly share some of your fondest memories and how the house enhanced those experiences. For example, in my last house the openness of the house facilitated wonderful household communication. Buyers can't actually see all the lifestyle features that a house facilitates. This letter brings a personal perspective to the house and gives the feeling of sharing an insider's secret. Have copies of the letter available for buyers to take with the feature sheet.

MAKE LEAVING FUN!

While there's no escaping the stress of showing your home, the spirit you want to create now is definitely F-U-N. To keep every member of the family—including you—passionately in the game until the happy ending, be creative about finding ways to keep spirits high. Here are a few suggestions of things to do while the house is being shown:

❑ Be a tourist in your own town: Visit the zoo or the science museum; take the garden tour at the botanical society. Be well prepared, by having all the schedules, fees, and other details on hand, so each time that unexpected call comes and you need to leave the house, you'll have an activity to suggest that everyone will enjoy.

❑ Say good-bye. Chances are time will be short once a sale contract is signed and you become preoccupied with moving. So if you're leaving a city or a neighborhood, now is an ideal time for some relaxed leave-taking.

❑ Of course, every showing can't find you all trekking to a museum or garden tour. There will be times when you won't be able to plan much. Keep a stack of books for you and the kids to read, and some games and puzzles (as if for a long car trip), so you have some things to do in the park or at a neighbor's house for the forty-five minutes you'll be away from the house.

EASING THE TRANSITION

There is a buyer for every house. So if your house doesn't sell on the very first day, relax! Your efforts will be rewarded soon with a profitable sale. The demands and frustrations of this period put a strain on every member of the household. That's why it's important to take a proactive role right now. Pave the way for a smooth move by beginning to disengage emotionally from your house to bring your experiences full circle.

✔ Start a photo journal with your children. Take pictures of them with their neighborhood friends. Create a book and use your house's address as the title: *My Adventures at 324 Willow Lane.* Make a poster for your children with photos, names, and telephone numbers of old friends.

✔ Rent a camcorder and make a "home video"—*Life at 324 Willow Lane.*

✔ Have an Open House farewell party. Make it a "bring your own" to keep life simpler.

✔ Take time for more intimate good-byes with friends, whether it's a long lunch while your house is being shown, a leisurely Saturday-morning walk through the neighborhood, or one last game of catch with a favorite pal.

✔ Start packing. Stack packed boxes neatly in the garage or another out-of-the-way spot.

✔ Get going on the details of a move. Contact new schools. Transfer medical and dental records.

✔ Spend time together. Just being together helps reduce the stress. Rent a movie, play a game.

❑ Finally, celebrate. When you are able to be home together, when you're fairly certain that a showing won't suddenly come up, plan celebrations around a family meal. Be sure to recognize the award winners from your most-innovative and best-attention-to-details contests. Hand out lots of recognition for everybody's contribution. Especially if your house is on the market for an extended period, you'll need to appreciate everyone's effort along the way—and keep the spirit of fun alive until you have something really big to celebrate together.

Remember, while the demands and frustrations of having a house on the market can put a strain on every member of the household, there are personal benefits to having a house in ShowTime condition, too. Think about how great it feels to come home to a sparkling clean and orderly house. That's the feeling of ShowTime. It's just one of the many rewards you'll experience from the effort you've put into your house over the last ten days.

THE SALE OF A LIFETIME

In a perfect world, life's transitions go according to plan. Finding a new home, for example, occurs immediately after your current home is sold. The actual move occurs right after that.

In the real world, however, events unfold more randomly. Your decision to move might be related to your job, or you might suddenly find the house of your dreams. Only then do you take the steps necessary to prepare your current house for sale.

Whatever the sequence of events, this program will improve both the process and the outcome. It helps you take a hard look at the myriad possessions you forgot you owned and allows you to remove the clutter, so that when the time actually comes to move, your packing will be much lighter!

You'll also see your house in an entirely new way—as a marketable product. While the house is on the market, you'll have time to disengage and take your leave: to bid farewell to the house, the neighborhood, even the town or region—to gradually and comfortably say good-bye (see the box on page 168).

During the intense preparation, you've been able to pull your family together toward one goal. You've probably built a sense of team spirit and a feeling and way of working together that will be a real asset as you start a new life in a new location.

A standing ovation for the cast.

Best of all, if you've adopted the program described in this book, you have enjoyed a sense of personal achievement. You have more money in your bank account than you ever expected —money that will make a difference in your transition to a new life in a new home.

APPENDICES

Welcome To

123 Monroe Street
Western Hills
$###,###

An Outstanding Family Home in Chicago's Western Suburbs
15 Minutes from Downtown, Ridgedale, Southdale
in the Nationally Acclaimed Western Hills School District
Nestled in the Prime "Riverdale" Neighborhood

*A floor plan that brings the outdoors in
and facilitates family interaction in a
casual living atmosphere.*

FEATURES

❑ **A Fabulous Backyard for Family Fun & Entertaining.**
Three sets of patio doors and full-wall windows open
the back of the home to a spacious wood deck,
screened gazebo, patio, in-ground concrete pool with
new sand filter. New fence. Professionally landscaped.
Mature perennial garden.

- **Gourmet Euro-Kitchen with Ceramic Tile Floor & Counters.** Two ovens (1 Jenn-Air range with convection combo; 1 built-in with microwave), dishwasher, disposal, compactor. Cooking island, rollouts. Eating area with 2 skylights.

- **Master Suite with Freestanding Fireplace on Marble Inset.** Walk-in closet, white tile dressing room, bath with double sink, rollout vanity, steam shower, Jacuzzi, and 3 skylights.

- **Oak-Paneled Library/Office.** (Possible 4th bedroom)

- **Living Room & Dining Room.** Feature 2 walls of windows and marble fireplace.

- **Four-Season Porch/Family Room.** With 3 walls of windows.

- **Berber Carpeting throughout First Floor.**

- **Original Knotty-Pine Amusement Room.** Fireplace, new carpeting, new recessed lighting and ceiling, wet bar/kitchenette.

- **Central Air, Humidifier, Double Attached Garage, 2 Furnaces.**

Appendix B:

The Dress Your House for Success ShowTime Game

Keep a running tally of each family member's contributions to keeping your house ShowTime ready. Use a separate score card for each, as in the sample below, and dole out prizes according to the chart at right at the end of each week.

Example:

Name	Chore Description/Points		MON	TUE	WED
WHITNEY	Make bed	2	2	2	2
	Pick up toys	1	1	1	—
	Put away toothbrush	1	1	1	1
	Hang up towels	1	1	—	1
	Put soda cans in recycle bin	1	1	1	—
	Pick up Sports Section	1	1	1	1
	Put away saxophone	1	1	1	1
	Mow lawn	3	—	—	—
	Take out recycling	2	—	—	2
	Daily bonus for completing all jobs	2	2	—	—
	Total Points		10	7	8

Name	Chore Description/Points		MON	TUE	WED
	Daily bonus for completing all jobs				
	Total Points				

Prize	# Points
Rent movie of your choice	50
Veto power at prime time	75
Give chore to another person	75
Go out for ice cream	50

THR	FRI	SAT	SUN	Weekly Total
2	—	2	2	
1	1	1	1	
1	1	1	1	
1	—	1		
1	1	1	1	
1	1	1	1	
1	1	1	—	
—	3	—	—	
—	—	—	—	
2	—	2	—	
10	8	10	6 =	59

THR	FRI	SAT	SUN	Weekly Total

APPENDIX C:
The Garage Sale—Have It Now!

You probably don't view the mountain of material possessions collecting in your home as a gold mine . . . but it is! There is big money in the clutter in your basement, bedrooms, garage, and attic, not to mention your closets, drawers, bookshelves, desks, and storage boxes, which are full of all sorts of excess belongings that can be turned into cash.

The more ruthless you are in Uncluttering, the better your garage sale merchandise. Merchandise for a profitable garage sale can be anything from clothes you no longer wear to furniture that's lost its glow, to duplicate kitchen utensils, appliances, tools, lamps, even doors, rugs, and mattresses. Garage sales thrive on the outgrown stuff of childhood: skates, books, CDs, toys, game cartridges, board games, and on and on. With a well-organized and well-publicized garage sale, you can turn the clutter and the extras into a trip to the bank.

Good garage sales don't just happen. They are the result of positioning and packaging. The outcome of your garage sale will depend on a few key preparation steps and a plan, but it's relatively easy, it involves the whole family, and it's fun.

After selecting your inventory—you accomplished that while Uncluttering—there are three steps to a successful garage sale. First, publicity, promotion, and advertising are required to make people aware of your garage sale. The more people you pull in, the more you'll sell.

Second, there's the creation of your temporary store: preparing the sale space, the merchandise, and your staff (you and your family). Set an enticing stage for your garage sale—the better organized and more professional it looks, the more people will stop and the more money you stand to make.

Then there's the sale day: making it a fun experience for you and your household and maintaining your sense of humor through the whole affair.

1. PUBLICITY/PROMOTION/ADVERTISING: GENERATING TRAFFIC

Draw shoppers to your garage sale by getting the word out in as many ways as possible. Make sure your publicity efforts—newspaper advertising, flyers, and signs—jump out at your audience. Your goal is to make your sale distinguished from the dozens of other sales planned for that weekend. Convince garage-sale fanatics and skeptics alike that your sale is not to be missed.

First, decide on a catchy headline for all your publicity efforts. Choose descriptive words that communicate the quality and size of your sale: *A-1, first-rate, unique, prime, superior, enormous, grand, huge, blockbuster,* and more. Try "SAKS ON MONROE STREET," or use words to immediately distinguish the size and quantity of your sale: "COLOSSAL MOVING SALE." The words *moving sale* as opposed to *tag sale* give the impression of higher-quality goods, extras that simply don't fit in your new house rather than discards.

Newspaper Advertising

When and How Much: Classified ads are a cost-effective way of getting the word out about your sale. Advertise in both city and local newspapers to reach the biggest audience. Garage-sale lovers, dealers, and professionals scour classifieds to plan their shopping itinerary. Invest in a slightly larger ad to stand out from the typical three-to-five-line ads, and run it two days before and the day of your sale. The investment of $40 to $90 is good insurance that a broad group of shoppers will know about your sale.

Content: Grab attention with your headline. If your newspaper runs ads alphabetically by headline, start with the letter *A* as in "A-1 TOP QUALITY GARAGE SALE" and it will appear first under garage-sale listings. If your budget permits, use a border to set the ad apart. Lead with your star items like an antique dining table, child's bedroom set, Rollerblades, and include categories of items: antiques, collectibles, patio furniture, camping equipment, children's clothing. Choose categories that will attract a variety of shoppers. Include a brief phrase describing where the items are from, like "5-FAMILY SALE" or "THREE GENERATIONS."

Next, give an overall description of your inventory with words and phrases like *high caliber, fine, quality products, no junk.* Complete your ad with the date, exact times, and address of the sale. Don't list the telephone number. Callers will only interrupt your sale preparations trying to beat other shoppers to the best items.

* * * * *

GIGANTIC MONROE STREET MOVING SALE
Antique mahogany dining table, silver, sewing machine, youth beds, top-quality housewares, children's clothes, games, books, tools, lawn furniture, camping equipment and more! Quality items from 5 families. FREE COFFEE. Sat. June 7, 8–3. 123 Monroe St., Western Hills; 1 blk. south of Hwy. 19 & 8th Ave.

* * * * *

Flyers

Promotional flyers are easy and inexpensive to produce. Use your headline, expand the text from your classified ad, and add a map at the bottom of an 8½-by-11-inch sheet of paper. Make copies on brightly colored paper for added impact. In addition to posting them in local stores, supermarkets, on community bulletin boards and utility poles, send family members door-to-door in your neighborhood to put flyers inside screen doors. Handwrite a personal invitation: "Hope to see you Saturday."

Try a neighborhood Preview Party the night before the sale. You'll get a start on the sales, plus you'll have an opportunity to talk to friends at a less busy time than sale day.

Street Signs

Sale-day promotion is essential for success. Draw in buyers and browsers with large, easy-to-read street signs. Use the same headline on street signs that appears in your classified ad. Consistency and high quality pay off. The bigger, bolder, and more professional looking, the better. Avoid hand lettering. Use stencils or a computer to produce signs that communicate quality. Place a sequence of three or four signs in both directions on the main road running past your side street. On the side streets, you'll need additional signs or coordinated arrows, clearly pointing the way to your sale. You can draw bold arrows at the bottom of flyers to direct traffic. Professional signs are the most effective way of pulling in casual weekend drivers . . . by the carload!

2. SETTING THE STAGE FOR YOUR TEMPORARY STORE

Once you get shoppers to your driveway, getting them to stop and look will depend on eye-catching displays. Enhance the overall presentation of your garage sale with attractive table coverings and clean, well-displayed items in a festive environment. Concentrate on both the overall appearance of the sale as well as the condition of each individual item. Enticing appearance and great condition enhance value.

Create the *feeling* of an outdoor fair at your garage sale. Tie a colorful bouquet of balloons to a tree or mailbox. Hang a string of "grand opening" type flags from the top of your roof right down to the front lawn. Play music to add to the festivities.

Dress all sale helpers in the same color shirt or matching baseball hats so they're highly visible. Put a sticker on each that says "I'm here to help" or "Make me an offer."

Set up an old-fashioned lemonade and snack stand on the driveway and encourage customers to linger and browse. Have children decorate it with eye-catching signs, streamers, balloons, and more! Put them in charge. Kids' enthusiasm is infectious. Before long, everyone will be sipping lemonade, munching on doughnuts, and buying, buying, buying.

Condition, Condition, Condition

Make sure your merchandise is in great condition. Naturally, a bright, shiny coffeemaker is more salable than a dingy, dirty one. Clean all your sale items—whether old or not—until they sparkle like new. Be meticulous. Use a household cleaner to scrub every item and then polish to a shine with glass cleaner. Wash clothes and fabric items. Tri-fold clothes for a more appealing look and put sizing labels on everything. Run dishes through the dishwasher. Group together and label sets. For example, eight glasses, ten plates; tie sets of sheets and towels together with ribbons; size-label curtains and put in dry-cleaning bags; use plastic food bags to hold items with parts. Place electronic equipment such as TVs and radios near a power source so shoppers can test their condition. The better the condition of your merchandise, the more quickly and profitably it will sell. Similarily, the more attractive it looks, the more buyers are willing to pay.

Setting Up

Make sure there is plenty of display space and showcase your merchandise in the same way retail stores do. Tables are essential; don't lay items on the lawn. Borrow or rent enough to display items without stacking. Organized tables encourage customers to browse. Crowded tables make your inventory look like clutter and less valuable. Group items by category, each with its own table, and arrange for visual interest. Identify each grouping with well-marked signs: "ANTIQUES," "HOUSEWARES," "SPORTING GOODS," etc.

Further encourage browsing with ample space between tables so buyers can walk around and between. Make sure larger, more notable items like an antique china cabinet, a sofa, or a child's swing set are visible from the road to attract customers.

Set up a special "BARGAIN" nook—what may seem dated or defunct to you can be a long-sought-after treasure to another. While preparing for our last sale, I found dozens of plastic potting pots and hanging planters that I'd forgotten to throw away. Rather than toss them, I grouped them with some old clay pots in a special bargain area. They sold to a home gardener who was thrilled to find such a bargain.

Get kids involved with a "KIDS ONLY" section stocked full of toys and treasures for small shoppers on small budgets. The chance to earn real cash often encourages kids to sell their underutilized toys and outgrown clothes. Children love to take part in garage sales and get really excited about being in charge of their *own* area.

Pricing

There's absolutely no formula for garage sale pricing. As you thoroughly clean each item, decide what you would be willing to pay if you were the buyer. You really can't go wrong. If you have no idea at all, visit garage sales in your area to see what similar items are selling for. Look carefully at condition; it's the key factor in pricing. The better the condition, the higher you can price it. People will pay more for an item in "like new" condition.

Use bright-colored stickers or labels on every item so the prices are easy to see. (We use color-coded stickers for each family member and divide profits at day's end.) For unusual items, write a brief description—what it does, how to use it, the price, and any special features—on an attractive notecard and attach it to the item.

3. SALE DAY DETAILS

Be prepared for an onslaught. A well-publicized sale will bring eager shoppers and dealers knocking on your door earlier than starting time. At my last garage sale, I was still sleeping when the doorbell rang! It is difficult to keep them at bay, so arrange tables the day before the sale. That way, you can begin selling as soon as you open the garage door. If you don't want to start selling early, be firm and ask shoppers to wait until you are set up.

Update Throughout the Day

After a rush of customers, recheck your set. Make sure the tables look enticing, items are well identified, price tags are visible. Remerchandise your tables as the day progresses: Refold and stack items, consolidate tables to avoid a picked-over look, and spread out merchandise for easier viewing. As it sells, replace inventory in the front of the sale where it's easily seen from the road. Many customers drive by a sale to see if there's anything interesting. If something catches their eye, they come in for a closer look; if not, they keep on driving. You want to pull in buyers throughout the day.

THE ART OF THE DEAL

Be prepared to bargain. Many shoppers approach garage sales as an invitation to negotiate. "Two dollars each! I'll pay you three dollars for both." Listen to buyers' requests, engage in a cheerful dialogue, and remember, the point of your sale is to get rid of clutter and sell out at day's end. Expect canny shoppers to arrive or return at the end of the day for "a deal."

Remain open, enthusiastic, and cheery. Actively approach every person who sets foot on your driveway. Extend a warm, friendly welcome, introduce yourself, and point out a few special items. Ask if they are looking for something in particular. Encourage customers to enjoy a lemonade and browse. Direct children to the KIDS ONLY section. Encourage shoppers to touch, try on, hold, and examine the merchandise. Near the end, offer

TIPS FOR SALE DAY

✔ Be ready early. A well-promoted sale attracts eager buyers.

✔ Lock your house. Don't let customers go inside for any reason.

✔ Have plenty of change in a belt pack worn on your body, not a change box that sits on a table.

✔ Keep a power cord handy for shoppers to test electrical purchases.

✔ Have a marker and extra price stickers in your belt pack for replacing lost prices and for late-day markdowns.

✔ Plan meals and snacks for helpers.

✔ Have several calculators on hand to speed up checkout.

✔ Set up a wrapping or bagging area next to the checkout table. Kids love to wrap and bag. If you don't have extra helpers, make it a wrap-your-own table.

✔ If it doesn't sell, don't keep it. Call a charitable organization to pick up what's left. Be sure to get a receipt for tax purposes.

discounts for multiple purchases, give small toys to children, and cut prices on what remains. The last hour of the day I discount prices by 50 percent. The object is to sell out, not haul away leftover merchandise.

RECYCLE FOR PROFIT

Orchestrating a garage sale fuels the spirit of entrepreneurship. It enables you to be in business for yourself—being in charge of the process is especially rewarding when the profits are yours to keep. The feeling of pride and accomplishment at the end of sale day is exhilarating. You've not only gotten rid of excess clutter, you've encouraged recycling and transformed unwanted items into usable cash. Instead of filling junkyards, goods sold at garage sales help fuel the economy. Garage sales are as healthy for the environment as they are for individual lifestyles and pocketbooks.

Enjoy the success. You've earned it.

INDEX